**Richards**       Scarab Seals from a Middle to Late Bronze Age
                   Tomb at Pella in Jordan

# ORBIS BIBLICUS ET ORIENTALIS

Published by the Biblical Institute of the University
of Fribourg Switzerland
the Seminar für Biblische Zeitgeschichte
of the University of Münster i.W. Federal Republic of Germany
and the Schweizerische Gesellschaft
für orientalische Altertumswissenschaft
Editor: Othmar Keel
Coeditors: Erich Zenger and Albert de Pury

*About the author*

Graduate of the University of Sydney, Australia, 1986 and currently engaged in research into the 'anra' scarabs at the University of Edinburgh for the degree of Ph. D. Core staff member of the University of Sydney excavations at Pella of the Decapolis, Jordan, from 1984 to 1990. Team member of the Egypt Exploration Society's expedition to Memphis, Egypt, 1987 and the excavations at Tell el–Dab'a, Egypt with the Institute of Egyptology, University of Vienna, 1989. Participant of the joint project between the University of Swansea, Wales and the University of Leiden, Belgium at Sagalassis, Turkey, 1989.

Orbis Biblicus et Orientalis    117

Fiona V. Richards

# Scarab Seals from a Middle to Late Bronze Age Tomb at Pella in Jordan

Universitätsverlag Freiburg Schweiz
Vandenhoeck & Ruprecht Göttingen

Die Deutsche Bibliothek – CIP-Einheitsaufnahme

**Richards, Fiona V.:**
Scarab Seals from a Middle to Late Bronze Age Tomb at Pella in Jordan / Fiona
V. Richards. – Freiburg, Schweiz: Univ.-Verl.; Göttingen: Vandenhoeck und
Ruprecht, 1992
   (Orbis biblicus et orientalis; 117)
   ISBN 3-525-53751-4 (Vandenhoeck und Ruprecht)
   ISBN 3-7278-0813-6 (Univ.-Verl.)
NE: GT

Publication subsidized by
the Swiss Academy of Humanities, Berne

© 1992 by Universitätsverlag Freiburg Schweiz
   Vandenhoeck & Ruprecht Göttingen
   Paulusdruckerei Freiburg Schweiz

ISBN 3-7278-0813-6 (Universitätsverlag)
ISBN 3-525-53751-4 (Vandenhoeck & Ruprecht)

FOR P.M.R.
*with love*

# ACKNOWLEDGEMENTS

I wish to thank the following for their help in the publication of the Pella scarabs:

Professor Basil Hennessy for his kind permission to publish the scarabs from Tomb 62 and Professor Harry Smith for his generous help with the hieroglyphs and the manuscript.

I would also like to thank Professor Othmar Keel for his generosity in giving me permission to publish the scarab from Schamir, Dr. Adnan Hadidi, former Director of the Antiquities Department in Jordan, and Dr. Piotr Bienkowski Curator, Egyptian and Near Eastern Antiquities at the Liverpool Museum for allowing me access to the scarabs.

Dr Ian Threadgold, Geogology and Geophysics Department, University of Sydney and Dr. Margaret Elcombe, Australian Institute of Nuclear Science and Engineering kindly helped with the analysis of the scarab material. Dr. John Powell of the British Geological Survey gave expertise knowledge of geological matters.

With regard to the drawing/ inking of the Pella scarabs I wish to thank Dr. Lisa Giddy, although special appreciation must go to Miss Justine Channing who was responsible for most of them. Mr Russell Workman kindly photographed all the scarabs.

Finally, I would like to thank the following for their help and involvement with the project, past and present: Miss Christa Mlinar, Dr. Alan Walmsley, Mrs Maree Browne, Miss Ana Tavares, Dr. Louise Maguire and last but not least, Mr Stephen Bourke for his unfailing encouragement and enthusiasm.

# CONTENTS

# LIST OF FIGURES IN TEXT

xi

# 1. INTRODUCTION

During the course of excavations of Area XI at Pella, a large multi-period site located in the Jordan Valley[1], fifty-five scarabs were recovered from a large Middle Bronze/Late Bronze Age (MB/LB) tomb. All scarabs were unmounted, and because of the water disturbance and reuse of the tomb, no useful contextual evidence can be provided, i.e. positioning on fingers, around necks and so forth.

The Pella scarabs represent an important group of seals, whose style is commonly associated with the Second Intermediate Period (SIP) in Egypt[2]. This catalogue of the scarabs offers a brief discussion regarding problems relating to the scarab seal as a useful archaeological tool, current typological trends, parallels, origins of manufacture and cultural significance.

## 1.1 PREVIOUS PUBLICATIONS

During the last ten years there have been a number of publications on various types of scarab seals[3]. It is not necessary to reiterate those

---

[1] For information on the excavations at Pella see McNicoll/Smith/Hennessy 1982, McNicoll et alii (in press).

[2] During the course of this paper, the term "Hyksos" is often used generically. Chronologically, the "Hyksos" are associated with the latter half of the SIP, or the Palestinian MBIIC period, i.e. 1650–1540BC.

[3] Of importance are Ward 1978, Tufnell 1984, Martin 1971, Hornung and Staehelin 1976. The OBO series has produced a number of recent publications: Keel/ Schroer 1985; Giveon 1985; Giveon 1988; Keel/Keel-Leu/Schroer 1989.

1

publications: the history and use[4] of the scarab seal is now well documented[5].

However, with interest and the number of publications on scarab seals increasing during recent years, a new problem has arisen: the establishment of a compatibility among scarab typologies. The scarab seal has the capacity to serve as an important relative chronological indicator for the archaeologist. However, this use is often undermined, because of the problems in establishing a coherent typology.

Petrie offered the first systematic grouping of scarab features (although concentrating on the base design) as early as 1889, and since that time many other typologies have been undertaken. Of note are those offered by Rowe, Martin, O'Connor[6], and Ward and Tufnell. Although all make reference to head, back and side types, it is the last study which offers the most through typology. That is, Ward and Tufnell were the first to consider five different criteria of the scarab seal, its dimensions, head, back, side and base design. This comprehensive study of all scarab features has underlined the utility of the seal both chronologically and stylistically[7].

Ward and Tufnell also recognised the difference between royal–name

---

[4]   See Giveon 1985, 9–14 for a good general discussion of the history of the scarab beetle; Ward 1978, Appendix D for a comment on the biological background of the *scarabaeus saucer*; Keel/Shuval/Uehlinger 1990, 259, n.389 for a discussion on the use of the seal.

[5]   Standard early publications include: Petrie 1917; 1925; Hall 1913; Newberry 1906; 1907. Early analyses of scarab seals of the Middle Kingdom and Second Intermediate Period include: Weill 1953, and Stock 1942.

[6]   Rowe 1936; Martin 1971 and O'Connor 1987.

[7]   Although not all may agree with Ward and Tufnell's chronological conclusions, their methodology is pioneering.

typologies and design scarab typologies. It is often not made clear that there are in fact, three different types of scarabs: design, royal–name and private–name. Problems occur chronologically when one typology, usually associated with royal–names, is applied to another, most often design scarabs. As Ward notes,

> "the typology of these three categories does not necessarily coincide in any given period and may indeed be quite different...the design scarab should provide the basic typology and the royal–name scarabs help to establish the absolute chronology"(Ward 1987, 508).

Thus flexible and versatile typologies, acknowledging the three different types of scarab seals that exist, must be established if the scarabs are to be of use chronologically. Ward and Tufnell (1978, 1984) offer the best solution to this problem to date. Therefore, their typology has been adopted and expanded where necessary for the Pella scarabs (see Appendix A).

## 1.2   TOMB 62[8]

Tomb 62 is located on the northeast crest of Tell Husn. It consists of three rock cut chambers which are entered through a short dromos. The roofs of both chambers 1 and 2 had completely collapsed, while that of chamber 3 had partially collapsed, leaving many of the objects intact. With over 2,000 objects recovered from the tomb, it is the richest tomb discovered at Pella and one of the largest tombs excavated in the Levant.

The contents consisted of a normal domestic assemblage of jars, bowls,

---

[8]   For a full account of Tomb 62 and its contents see Potts in McNicoll et alii (in press), and Potts/Colledge/Edwards 1985.

jugs and lamps in buff, white and red slip wares which find their best parallels in the East Cut, phase 6 material on the site itself (Bourke in Hennessy 1989). A significant quantity of chocolate–on–white ware was found including jars, open bowls, cylindrical juglets, amphoriskoi and carinate bowls[9].

Besides the typical Transjordanian and Palestinian types there were also Cypriot and Syrian imports: these included a number of globular Black Lustrous Wheel Made Ware juglets, a Monochrome ware bowl and a Red Lustrous Wheel Made Ware spindle bottle[10].

The smaller objects included three cylinder seals; copper, bronze and one gold toggle pins, gold ear–rings, arrow–heads, glass beads, bone inlay incised with geometric designs from wooden boxes, bone spindle whorls and calcite flasks.

The tomb contents were distributed between the three chambers. Preliminary analysis has indicated approximately 150 individuals were buried in the tomb, the later burials being pushed to the rear of the chambers. This, coupled with the rock fall and water damage (water had washed or seeped into the tomb moving the contents) make any clear vertical stratification and contextual evidence for the scarabs difficult.

However, the date of the tomb has not been difficult to discern as most of the pottery represents familiar MBIIC/LBI styles, which is generally supported by the presence of Dynasty XV/ XVII scarabs.

---

[9]  See Hennessy 1985, for discussion of chocolate–on–white ware.

[10]  See Maguire 1991, Eriksson 1992 (forthcoming) for discussion on the origins of Red Lustrous Wheel Made Ware.

## 1.3   MATERIAL

The majority of scarabs discovered in Tomb 62 are made from the same material, and when first examined it was unclear whether the material was steatite or faience. Steatite is known to be the most popular material for the manufacture of scarabs used from the beginning of the industry. Faience was popular at the beginning of seal making in Egypt, but then died out. It had a resurgence in popularity in the New Kingdom[11]. There are three small, crudely made scarabs (**CN 49, p. 128/129, pl.XII;**[12] **CN 50, p.128/129, pl.XII; CN 51, p.130/131, pl.XII**) which are easily identifiable as faience[13], but opinion differed as to the material used for the remaining scarabs.

Initial tests on the Pella scarabs employed the x–ray diffraction technique. This involved the scarabs being subjected to an x–ray beam which provides a graph showing the diffraction of the crystalline substance of the scarab[14].

A Phillips PW 1050/70 x–ray powder diffractometer was used in conjunction with a Phillips PW 1730 x–ray generator, a PW 1373 gorimeter supply, a PW 1390 channel control and a PM 8203 chart recorder. The x–ray technique requires a flat surface to be irradiated with a divergent x–ray beam; once the specimen is struck, if crystalline, produces a diffraction of the beam and eventually a

---

[11]   See Ward 1978, 34ff and Tufnell 1984, 42.

[12]   CN = Catalogue Number within this publication; page numbers refer to descriptions and drawings within the 'Catalogue' section, p.79ff.

[13]   **CN 53 (p.132/133, pl.XII)** is burnt and badly blistered but is also thought to be of faience.

[14]   This work involved the kind co–operation of Dr Ian Threadgold of the Department of Geology and Geophysics at the University of Sydney.

diffractogram[15]. Once the diffractogram is obtained, the peaks should be easily identifiable by measuring each pattern which can then identify the crystalline phase that produced the pattern.

The scarabs analysed produced a multi–phase system which meant that the peaks were difficult to identify because each phase with its characteristic peaks was superimposed on another. However, it was apparent that there were a number of peaks common to several scarabs.

It was immediately clear that the scarabs analysed were not made of faience. Faience is a mixture of alkali and quartz, like glass, which means that it is amorphous – non crystalline. If the scarabs tested had been made of faience, then peaks would not have been produced on any of the graphs, and all showed peaks.

As there was difficulty in identifying the x–ray diffraction peaks, a small amount of material was subsequently removed from a broken scarab for further analysis by the x–ray diffraction technique, but this time using the film technique. The x–ray powder photograph obtained using CuKα radiation revealed the presence of orthopyroxene enstatite $(Mg_2(SiO_3)_2)$.

The fact that the major peaks of the diffractogram could not be identified, indicated that after being carved, the scarabs had undergone further treatment, which changed the composition and mineralogy of the outer layers. It was also noted that the inner material of the scarabs

---

[15] Any crystalline structure is made up of planes which are set at a certain interval, and the perpendicular spacings between the planes are known as the 'd' spacings. The peaks produced on a diffractogram are the result of the x–ray beams that hit the planes and are diffracted. (The x–ray beam however, will only be diffracted when certain conditions are satisfied). Each crystalline compound, by virtue of its three dimensional periodic arrangements of its atoms, has a unique set of diffraction peaks, the position and intensity of which characterise it, rather like a finger–print (pers. comm. Threadgold 1985).

was soft. It was later confirmed that heated steatite is enstatite, and that the heating of the steatite would have caused the identifying pattern of the peaks to change[16].

Further tests have been initiated to confirm this initial response, and to try and identify the source of the material which would be invaluable to our knowledge of trade networks at this time. One of the major problems with the above technique was the inability of the atoms to pass through the outer surface of the scarab to the inner core. Thus there was a danger of it identifying the outer, often glazed or heated material rather than the original composition.

To this end, a similar technique was employed, now capable of penetrating the scarab exterior to analyse the inner material without damaging the artifact in any way. Ten scarabs were analysed in a trial examination, using the neutron diffraction method, as neutrons provide the ideal tool for probing material without causing damage. In 1989, neutron diffraction patterns were analysed which differentiated three distinct internal materials. A high resolution diffraction pattern was then taken, further helping the analysis of such material[17].

Thus far, the most common material of the scarabs at Pella appears to be steatite, a naturally occurring soap stone, which can be carved easily. Steatite does not occur naturally in ancient Palestine, but does occur in the mountain region of Syria and in large quantities in Cyprus and is also found in Egypt.

Three further materials were used in the manufacture of the Pella scarabs. **CN 52 (p.130/131, pl.XII)** is made of amethyst, a clear

---

[16]   This is the same result that Tufnell received when she analysed two examples from the British Museum (Tufnell 1984, 42).

[17]   My thanks to Dr Margaret Elcombe of the Australian Institute of Nuclear Science and Engineering, for all her help with this project. Further funds have been allocated for the analysis of the remaining Pella material.

pinky/purple colour. Amethyst is known to be a material used in the manufacture of scarab seals, but it is quite rare, and does not seem to have been used before the XIIth Dynasty, and only in a few cases since then[18].

Another rare material is wood, and there is one example (**CN 55, p.134/135, pl.XIII**) of this material at Pella. Hall notes that wood is one of the first materials used in the manufacture of seals[19]; however, it was later abandoned, and there are only two published examples which exist from the XIIth and XXth Dynasties[20]. **CN 54 (p.132/133, pl.XIII),** is made from a polished green stone, identified as enstatite[21].

## 2.   PARALLELS

When researching parallels for the designs on the Pella scarabs, over 30 sites in Nubia, Egypt, Palestine and Syria[22] were considered, and

---

[18]   Ward 1978, 84–86.

[19]   Hall 1913, p.xxviii

[20]   See Petrie 1917, 12.2.5 from the XIIth Dynasty, Senusert I; and Rowe 1936, no. 853, from Tell en Nasbeh, c. XXth Dynasty or later, from T.32 of the Western Cemetery, south strip.

[21]   Courtesy of Dr. Ian Threadgold, Geology and Geophysics, University of Sydney.

[22]   The discussion on parallels is therefore based on the following sites: Ugarit, Byblos, Tell Keisan, Sidon–Ruweise, Akko, Beth Shan, Tell Kabri, Tell Michal, Megiddo, Aphek, Hazor, Shechem, Tell Nagila, Hirbet Qara, Tell Jerishe, Tell Aviv, Hasorea, Gezer, Gibeon, Jericho, Tell Abu Zureiq, Ain Shems, Lachish, Tell el-'Ajjul, Tell Beit Mirsim, Beth Pelet, Tell Jemmeh, Khataneh, Ezbet Rushdi, Tell el–Dab'a, Kahun, Lahun, Gurob, Harageh, Tumas, Masmas, Uronarit, Aniba, Kerma, Ukma Ouest, Sai, Mirgissa.

several factors were taken into account regarding the design itself. That is, it was not sufficient for a parallel to only be of a similar type of design category (e.g. lion, human figure); the style of cutting of the design was also considered, as were the different compositional elements of the design[23].


## 2.1   ROYAL NAME SCARABS

Three scarabs have been included in this section, although only the first, Auserre Apophis, has been identified with any certainty[24]. The remaining two pieces, of Nubuserre and Kamose, have nevertheless been included here: there is no reason to doubt the former and although the latter is unusual, it should not be dismissed outright for lack of cartouche.

The first scarab (**CN 1, p.80/81, pl.I**), has a decorated back, simply rendered legs and unfortunately, a damaged head, leaving it unclassified. The base reads in transliteration: $^{c}3-wsr-r^{c}$ (Apophis). The hieroglyphs are written within a cartouche, with a $k_3$ positioned above. The cartouche is flanked by stylised lotuses and $^{c}n\underline{h}$ $nfr$ is placed at the sides.

To date there is only one exact parallel to the base of this scarab[25].

---

[23]   E.g. CN 6 has two figures with ambiguous head types and bent knees. A scarab which just exhibits two figures would not be considered as a 'close' parallel (Keel 1989, p.225, fig.27 or Schroer 1985, p.95, fig.68, 70). Neither would those that exhibit falcon heads (Reisner 1923, pl.40:II–89) or distinctive human heads (Loud 1984, pl.150:71). A 'close' parallel is one that exhibits the same head type, stance and dress as much as possible.

[24]   My thanks to Professor Smith and Professor Martin (University College London) for their advice on the royal–name scarabs (pers. comm.). Any final decision regarding their classification however, remains my own.

[25]   Tufnell 1984, Vol II: no. 3451 from a collection, Spencer Churchill.

This includes the cartouche, hieroglyphs and surrounding elements. Unfortunately there is no context for this scarab.

Auserre Apophis is one of the better known and documented 'Hyksos' rulers[26]. He is attested to in literature by the Rhind Mathematical Papyrus, the Papyrus Sallier I, and the Kamose stelae. There is also a scribe's palette from the Fayyum with a dedication to Apophis, 'beloved of Re' which also bears the ancient title 'King of Upper and Lower Egypt'; an adze blade with an inscription to 'the good god 'Auserre, beloved of Sobk, Lord of Sumenu' and an alabaster vessel inscribed for his daughter, Princess Herit, was discovered in the tomb of Amenhotep I (Hayes 1973, 62). His throne name (twice repeated on either side of a winged sun disk) is found on a building block of granite from Gebelein. His name has also been found on a large number of scarabs.

It is clear from these records that Auserre Apophis was a contemporary of Kamose and that the war between Thebes and Avaris was completed ten years later under Amosis. It is known that Kamose campaigned against Auserre and plundered Auserre's fleet at the port of Avaris but failed to capture the city.

However, even with such good documentation, it is still debated in what position Auserre Apophis lies within the sequence of Hyksos kings. Von Beckerath and Ward[27] believe that Auserre Apophis lies in 5th position of the Turin Canon, while Hayes and Helck[28] place Apophis in 4th position.

---

[26] For the following list refer to Hayes 1973, 61–62 and van Seters 1966, 154–157.

[27] von Beckerath 1964, 127ff and Ward in Tufnell 1984, 162.

[28] Helck 1962, 133 and Hayes 1973, 61.

Outside Egypt, Apophis is known only by his scarabs, of which all four previously known examples come from Tell el-'Ajjul. Now, besides the Pella example, a further Apophis scarab has been found in the North of Palestine, at Schamir, near Dan (see fig. 1).

The second Royal Name scarab from Pella (**CN 2, p.80/81, pl.I**), has an 'open' type head, plain back and simply rendered legs represented by a single scored line. Its base reads in transliteration from top to bottom down the length of the scarab, '*ntr nfr Nbw−wsr−r di ᶜnḫ*' and is surrounded by a so-called Hyksos 'royal border' of the panel variety[29]. The hieroglyphs are a perfectly acceptable rendition of Nubuserre[30] and as Ward notes (Tufnell 1984, 164), the prenomen is always preceded by 'goodly god' and the common pharaonic epithet, 'given life' follows.

Two close parallels exist. One is from Moscow[31] with a base design that renders the *ntr* slightly differently and reverses the *di ᶜnḫ*. It has a plain back and simply depicted legs, although it has a 'lunate' head as opposed to the 'open' type displayed on the Pella scarab. The second parallel comes from the University College collection[32], and the only difference on the base is the depiction of the *wsr* sign. However, on both examples the number of cross strokes on the panel design differs and the first parallel also lacks a second vertical line. Unfortunately the

---

[29]  See Ward in Tufnell 1984, 165 for discussion on the 'Royal Border'. This border originated in the Middle Kingdom as the arrangement of pairs of hieroglyphs in two vertical columns. This design was virtually rare in the XIIIth Dynasty and only re-appeared in the Hyksos period with two vertical lines separating these pairs of signs from the name in the central panel.

[30]  Although it is not cited by von Beckerath 1984, 77–80, in his standard list of Kings.

[31]  Tufnell 1984, Vol II: no. 3487.

[32]  Tufnell 1984, Vol II: no.3491; UC 16587.

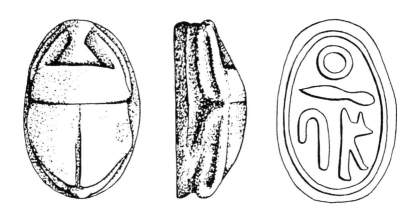

Fig.1   Apophis scarab from Shamir (near Dan), Upper Galilee


DIMENSIONS:        16.7 x 11.6 x 7.1 mm
MATERIAL:          Baked clay with traces of green glaze
LOCATION:          Found inside a 'dolmen' at the Kibbutz
                   Shamir
                   See plate xiii.56 for photographs

origin of the former scarab is unknown, and the scarab from University College was purchased by Petrie in Egypt.

Historically, little is known of Nubuserre. He is generally acknowledged to be a minor ruler who is known only from his scarab record. While many scholars make no reference to him at all,[33] Ward places him in his main sequence of XVth Dynasty kings (Tufnell 1984, 163), and von Beckerath with his lesser rulers of the XVIth Dynasty (1964, 139). According to Weinstein (1981, fig.2) there have been no scarabs of this ruler found to date in Palestine; so the Pella example would be the first.

The third Pella Royal Name scarab (**CN 3, p.82/83, pl.I**) is beautifully made, with fine detailed carving. It has a 'lunate' type head with a high, plain back and intricately feathered legs. The base consists of hieroglyphs running down the length of the scarab. The central column reads $w_3\underline{d}$ $-r^\varsigma-$ $hpr$ (to be read $w_3\underline{d}-hpr-r^\varsigma$) which is flanked by $Hr$ falcons, $nb$, $k_3$, $nb$; below is a double *ureaus* enclosing two *nfr* signs. The central column therefore provides the elements of Kamose's nsw-bity name, $w_3\underline{d}-hpr-r^\varsigma$, although in the incorrect order. However, its positioning in the central column of the base, and the fact that it is surrounded by 'royal' symbols might signify its intent as a royal name scarab.

An exact parallel for this scarab is found at Tell el-'Ajjul[34]. A second, similar scarab was also found at Tell el-'Ajjul[35] with the same central column and flanking designs, but with two red crowns at the bottom instead of *uraei*.

---

[33] Helck 1962, Van Seters 1972, Engberg 1939, Hayes 1973, & Stock 1942 make no reference to a $Nbw-wsr-r$ in the Hyksos Dynasty.

[34] Petrie, 1933: pl III:54, Tufnell 1984, Vol II: no.1485.

[35] Petrie 1931, pl.xiv:125, Tufnell 1984, Vol II: no.1566.

13

Historically, Kamose is well known from his stelae documenting his war against Apophis[36], although once again, none of his scarabs have been found to date outside of Egypt, the example from Tell el-'Ajjul not being acknowledged as his.

The scarab of Auserre Apophis illustrates a true rendering of the prenomen, and this is confirmed by its presence within a cartouche. The Nubuserre scarab also has a perfectly acceptable rendition of his prenomen which is always proceeded by 'goodly god' and the common pharaonic epithet 'given life', as is demonstrated on the Pella example. It, too, is surrounded by a common 'Hyksos' royal border. The titles, epithets and execution of the written names suggest an Egyptian manufacture is likely.

Only the Kamose scarab reading may be disputed. Although the elements of his *nsw-bity* name are certainly present, their incorrect ordering and the lack of cartouche or other generally accepted 'royal' border may raise legitimate doubts as to an Egyptian manufacture. However, it is common for a royal name to be positioned centrally to the base running vertically down the length of the scarab. This positioning of the elements of Kamose's prenomen would support it being intended as a royal name, which in turn is further supported by the surrounding *uraei* and *Horus* – signs commonly associated with royalty. The scarab is also of the finest quality and superior workmanship. These factors may be seen to support the identification as a 'royal document'.

## 2.2 DESIGN SCARABS

### 2.2.i HUMAN FIGURES

There are six different types of human figure designs from Tomb 62.

---

[36] See Habachi 1972, and Smith & Smith 1976, 48–76.

There are two of the 'naked goddess' type scarabs from Tomb 62, (**CN 4, p.82/83, pl.I; & CN 5, p.84/85, pl.I**). Both illustrate the same type of triangular 'trapezoidal' head, plain back and simply depicted legs. They depict standing, frontal facing bodies with arms hanging down by their sides. CN 4 illustrates the figure facing to the left, while CN 5 illustrates the figure facing to the right. Both designs are partially surrounded by a border of stylised palm branches.

Following the recent work of Winter (1983) and Schroer (1989), it has been demonstrated that there is a difference between those figures which stand with frontal torso, arms hanging by sides, head facing front, and those with the same stance but with their heads facing to the side. The former type is generally acknowledged to represent the Egyptian goddess 'Hathor', and the latter has been suggested as having a Syrian origin (Schroer 1989, 93–5).

Parallels for the Syrian 'naked goddess' from Pella are found at Tell el–'Ajjul, Jericho, Gezer, Aphek, Beth Pelet, Lachish, Pella and there are three from private collections[37].

This design clearly illustrates that there were variant local styles in Palestine. The Pella example, although no different in content is clearly unlike any of the other parallels in style.

Every parallel mentioned above, except for the one from Tell el–'Ajjul, is clearly surrounded by a 'palm branch' which is drawn either as the real object, a stylised rendition of the real object or as a border. It would seem therefore, that the branch was an integral part of the design.

---

[37] Petrie 1934, pl.v:109; Sydney University NB 52.641 = Schroer 1989, p.97 no.3; Giveon 1985, p.114 no.16 = Schroer 1989, p.97 no.6; Schroer 1989, p. 97 no.9; Starkey/ Harding 1932, pl.lxxiii:12 = Schroer 1989, p.97 no.11; Tufnell 1958, pl.30:47 = Schroer 1989, p.98 no.16. Private collections: three are from The Biblical Institute, Freiburg, Switzerland (see Schroer 1989 p.97 nos.12–14) and one published by Hornblower 1922, pl.21:14.

Although Tufnell notes that the surrounding palms are often reduced to 'mere nicks' (1984, 138), Schroer (1989) believes the palms original intentions can be seen on Syrian cylinder seal scenes, where they were related to scenes which illustrated the goddess unveiling herself. For example, Fig.2 illustrates two scenes where the seal cutters have already begun to misrepresent the veil and portray it as a branch (fig. 2.i) or a veil with leaves on top (fig.2.ii).

Schroer believes the branch became an important symbol in Palestine, more so than in Syria or Babylonia, because of its relationship to the original goddess and as a substitute for her. In Palestine, the goddess was worshipped in fact as a branch goddess because the branch or tree was interpreted as possessing the vital powers of the goddess[38].

The second human figured design (**CN 6, p.84/85, pl.II**) illustrates two figures of ambiguous head type, facing each other with knees seemingly slightly bent on top of a *nb* sign. This scarab has a 'trapezoidal' head type, plain back and simply presented legs.

The upright (as opposed to kneeling) double or twin figure are quite common, appearing at Tell el–'Ajjul, Tell Beit Mirsim, Lachish, Beth Pelet, Megiddo, Tell Abu Zuseiq, and Gezer as well as Kerma and Aniba although there are none from the main Egyptian sites[39].

Two main groups can be distinguished: those clearly influenced by

---

[38] Hestrin (1987, 1991) suggests an association of the branch goddess with the goddess Asherah.

[39] Petrie 1934, pl.v:115,119; Petrie 1952, pl.ix:17; Albright 1938, pl.28:9; Tufnell 1958, pl.39:325; Starkey/Harding 1932, pl.xliv:59; Loud 1948, pl.149:52, pl.150:71, pl.150:82; pl.151:116; Schroer 1989, 255, fig.27; Schroer 1985, 95, fig.69; Macalister 1912, pl.cciva:2; Reisner 1923, pl.40,41/II–89, Steindorff 1937, pl.55:66.

*Figure 2.i: Goddess unveiling*

*Figure 2.ii: Goddess holding veil*

17

Egypt, i.e. they exhibit triangular skirts and are falcon headed[40] and those clearly influenced by Canaan with the longer, tighter skirts and human heads[41].

The Pella design illustrates neither definitive human or falcon heads, although it is closer to the former than the latter. It falls between those which were clearly influenced either by Egypt or Canaan. There is only one example that has a similar ambiguous head style from Megiddo, and one example from Hasorea which has a figure with similar bent knee[42].

A third human figure design (**CN 7, p.86/87, pl.II**), portrays a standing female figure facing to the left holding an unknown object, possibly a stylised palm branch. The scarab has a triangular 'trapezoidal' style head with plain back and simply depicted legs by a single groove from front threading hole to rear.

The standing figure is a common design with different poses and filling ornaments, and can be found at many sites throughout Palestine and Egypt including Tell el-'Ajjul, Beth Pelet, Gezer, Lachish, Tell Jerishe, Tell Beit Mirsim, Jericho, Tell el-Yehudiyeh, Tell el-Dab'a, Akko and also in Syria at Byblos.

However, the number of *female*[43] standing figures is limited to half a dozen, from Beth Shan, Beth Pelet, Hirbet Qara, and two from

---

[40] e.g. Petrie 1934, pl.v, 115 & 119; Loud 1948, pl.150: 82; Reisner 1923, pl.40,41/II-89.

[41] e.g. Petrie 1952, pl.ix,17; Tufnell 1958, pl.39:325; Macalister 1912, pl.cciva:2.

[42] Loud 1948, pl.151:116, Schroer 1985, p.95, fig.69.

[43] This is, however, a subjective term.

private collections[44]. The Pella example is unlike any of these parallels. Although it is typical of the period with its overall 'Hyksos' style, due to the way it is actually incised it is without an exact parallel. The style of illustration is the same as CN 5, indicating a possible regional or site style.

The kneeling figure holding a palm is represented by two slightly different examples at Pella (**CN 8, p.86/87, pl.II; & CN 9 p.88/89, pl.II**). Both have triangular 'trapezoidal' head types, plain backs and simply depicted legs by a single line running from the front threading hole to rear. CN 8 depicts a kneeling figure with a hatched skirt holding a stylised palm leaf and leaning slightly backwards. CN 9 shows a kneeling figure again holding a very stylised plant and leaning slightly forwards. Both skirt and upper body are hatched.

This is a very common design of the SIP. Numerous examples are found at Tell el-'Ajjul, Megiddo, Lachish, Gezer, Beth Pelet, Jericho Tell el-Dab'a, Gurob and Mirgissa[45].

An unusual human figured design at Pella (**CN 10, p.88/89, pl.III**) illustrates a figure with raised arms with a *ḫpr* beetle and *nb* sign in front of the figure and a *uraeus* and *nb* sign behind it. It has a damaged head, plain back and triangular legs. Only two examples of figures with both arms raised are known in Palestine, from Tell Keisan and Jericho[46].

---

[44] Rowe 1936, no.180 = Schroer 1989, 100 no.54; Starkey/Harding 1932, pl.xliii:13, pl.xliv:58; Keel in Briend/Humbert 1980, 260 fig.59; Winter 1983, pl.152, 468.

[45] Petrie 1931, pl.xiii:74; pl.xiv:162; Petrie 1934, pl.vii:176; Petrie 1952, pl.ix:29; Loud 1948, pl.149:38; Tufnell 1958, pl.36:238; pl.39:326; Macalister 1912, pl.xxxv:14, Petrie 1930, pl.x:88; Kirkbride 1965, fig.294:17, fig.293:11; Mlinar (unpublished) nos.1027, 1042; Brunton/Engelhart 1927, pl.xxi:1; Vercoutter 1976, fig.7Be.

[46] Briend/ Humbert 1980, 261, fig:62; Kirkbride 1965, fig:301:8.

However, these slim figures are more reminiscent of the later New Kingdom figures, although Williams classifies it as a 'fanciful style' (Williams 1970). There are other examples of figures with a single raised arm from Tell el–Ajjul, Jericho, Akko and Ugarit[47] in what is known as the 'Baal posture,'[48] and can be compared to representations of this god who is more commonly known from Syrian cylinder seals.

**CN 11 (p.90/91, pl.III)** is a magnificent scarab with a 'trapezoidal' head, notched clypeus, decorated back and triangular legs. The base design consists of a (male?) figure seated on a chair with 'lion' paws as feet, who seems to be holding the hand of a standing (female?) figure. Both figures wear hatched Canaanite skirts. This scarab would appear to be unique in its composition.

There are examples illustrating seated figures from Tell Michal, Tell el–'Ajjul, Beth Pelet and Gezer[49]. All have the same 'lion' chair, but the scarabs from Gezer and Tell Michal represent only the single, seated figure, while the example from Tell el–'Ajjul depicts the seated figure holding the other figure by the ankle, upside–down and the scarab from Beth Pelet depicts one seated and one standing figure above a figure lying prostrate. The scarab from Tell Michal is engraved in a very similar manner to CN 11: the only scarab seemingly to do so. The head is also of exactly the same type (including the notched clypeus) and there is a similar branch design on the back. The scarab from Gezer also has a decorated back and notched clypeus. Tufnell makes no mention of the seated figures or those with arms raised.

---

[47] Petrie 1952, pl.ix:34,42; Kirkbride 1965, fig.301:17; Giveon/Kertesz 1986, 15 no.26; Schaeffer 1939, pl.v:3.2/16.

[48] See Keel 1989, 264 pls.70–75.

[49] Herzog/Rapp/Negba 1989, pl.75.2, fig.291.2; Petrie 1952, pl.ix:15; Petrie 1930, pl.xxii:235; Macalister 1912, pl.cciia:7.

A scaraboid (**CN 18, p.96/97, pl.V**) depicts a standing skirted figure on the obverse and a *ḫpr* beetle and cobra design on the reverse (see later discussion 2.2.ii). This type of standing figure faces to the right and wears a triangular skirt which is reminiscent of an Egyptian counterpart, rather than a tightly wrapped Canaanite contemporary. The figure faces an animal(s), primarily two cobras although sometimes a crocodile. Both animal and human figures are placed above a *nb* sign.

This design is distinguished by its 'cut–out' engraving style, similar to several animal designs discussed later. It is a fairly common design, appearing at six major Palestinian sites although only at a couple of sites in Egypt and one in Nubia.

The designs can be divided by the type of head displayed by the skirted figure. The Pella design has an ambiguous head type, which is only paralleled at two sites in Palestine: Megiddo and Lachish[50]. The best parallel to this design from Pella is found at Kataneh[51]. Other head types are divided between human, for example those at Gibeon, Jericho, Lachish, Tell el-'Ajjul and Beth Pelet[52], and those with falcon heads such as those from Tell el-'Ajjul, Beth Pelet, Tell el-Dab'a and Kerma[53].

---

[50]   Loud 1948, pl.151:146; Tufnell 1958, pl.36:233.

[51]   Naville 1890, pl. xix:11.

[52]   Pritchard 1963, fig.71:3; Kirkbride 1965, fig.291:14, fig.298:15; Tufnell 1958, pl.36:233; Petrie 1952, pl.ix:23,31; Starkey/Harding 1932, pl.xliv:69.

[53]   Petrie 1931, pl.xiv:165; Petrie 1930, pl.vii:46; Mlinar nos. 701,801; Reisner 1923, pl.40,/II–86.

## 2.2.ii ANIMAL FIGURES

There are eight animal figures among the design scarabs. They consist of common animal designs, popular during the SIP/ MBIIB/C, of lions, cobras, and antelopes.

The antelope, identified in recent studies as a goat[54], is a particularly frequently occurring design during the Hyksos period and there are three examples at Pella, CN 12, 13 and 14. Examples can be found at all major sites in Palestine; Shechem, Gezer, Jericho, Lachish, Tell el-'Ajjul, Tell Jemmeh, Beth Pelet, and also in Egypt at Tell el–Dab'a and Tell el–Yehudiyeh and in Nubia at Kerma and Mirgissa.

Tufnell notes (1984, 132) that the goat had its origins in the First Intermediate Period (FIP) and its first appearance in Palestine at Megiddo, carefully drawn with a spotted hide. At Tell el–Dab'a the earliest appearance of the antelope dates from Stratum G[55]. It differs from its Palestinian counterparts however, because the animal is drawn lying down with its antlers in the upright position. Within Palestine it is seen in MBIIB (Jericho group III) where its presentation has reached what becomes the conventional design: the animal is seen in profile, head usually to the right, set longitudinally on the plinth and filling the entire field except for some additions above the back.

Pella goats **CN 12 (p.90/91, pl.III)** and **CN 13 (p.92/93, pl.III)** reflect this conventionality. Both have damaged head types, plain backs and simply depicted legs by a single incision running from the front threading hole to rear. The base designs set the goats longitudinally down the length of the scarab with the animal seen in profile, its head facing to the right. CN 12 has a tree as filling in front of its front legs

---

[54]  See Keel 1990, 263ff for discussion on the identification of the 'antelope' as a goat.

[55]  Mlinar (unpublished), no.13.

while CN 13 has an 'ᶜ' sign as filling above its back.

There is a certain similarity of design on the scarabs from Jericho Lachish, Tell el-'Ajjul and Shechem but none exhibit the same execution of design as the Pella goats[56].

The 'spotted hide' design of Pella CN 13 is only repeated at three other sites, Tell el-'Ajjul, Gezer and Shechem[57]. The 'scored' body of CN 12 is not found elsewhere, although 'hatched' bodies are represented at Jericho (all three examples), Tell el-'Ajjul, Tell Jemmeh, Beth Pelet, Tell Nagila and at Tell el-Yehudiyeh[58].

A third scarab with a goat at Pella (**CN 14; p.92/93, pl.IV**), is quite different from its counterparts. This is mostly due to the way in which it has been deeply carved and glazed. Its features are noticeably different too: it has a 'trapezoidal' type head but a divided prothorax and elytra with the elytra again divided into two, usually indicative of a later date. It has 'triangular' legs. The base design is distinguished not only by the prominent deeply carved figure, but because it is lying down. Otherwise the antelope is set longitudinally, with its head to the right, and some sort of filling ornament above its back. It belongs to the 'Hyksos' period in its style of design, but the divisions of its back suggest a later date than the other goat designs[59], closer to the

---

[56] Kirkbride 1965, fig.293:17, fig.301:12, fig.302:20; Tufnell 1958, pl.36:224; Petrie 1931, pl.xiii:1,18; Petrie 1933, pl.iii:27; Petrie 1934, pl.v:112, pl.xi:405; Petrie 1952, pl.x:117; Horn 1973, fig.1:60.

[57] Petrie 1931, pl.xiii:1; Giveon 1985, 117 no.22; Horn 1973, fig.1:60.

[58] Petrie 1934, pl.v:112, pl.xi:405; Giveon 1985, 57 no.1; Petrie 1930, pl.xii:127; Petrie 1906, pl.vi:5; Amiran/Eitan 1965, fig.15:2.

[59] Mlinar (unpublished) proposes a sequence in which the deeply 'cut out' designs are later than those with outlines incised. This corresponds with the later stylistic features of the divided back.

beginning of the LB.

As well as the early example at Tell el-Dab'a, there are three other examples of goats lying down, and they are found at Lachish, Aphek and Tell el-'Ajjul[60].

The depiction of the lion is a common design throughout Palestine during the MBIIC, with examples found at all major sites. Pella has two examples, CN 15 and 16, which are unusual because the representation of the lion is very stylised. **CN 15 (p.94/95, pl.IV)** has a 'trapezoidal' type head, with a plain back and simply depicted legs which include indication of the rear leg. The design is set longitudinally down the length of the scarab filling the entire field. The lion faces to the left and has a cobra in front and behind, with the latter attached to the lion's tail. **CN 16 (p.94/95, pl.IV)** also has a trapezoidal head, although badly incised, with a plain back and simply depicted legs by a single incision running from front threading hole to rear. Once again the lion is set longitudinally down the length of the scarab with a cobra in front and behind, and the latter cobra is again attached to the lion's tail.

The stylised version of the lion at Pella (as opposed to the more realistic representation, c.g. at Lachish or Megiddo)[61] is not confined to this site, for there are similar examples at Tell Keisan, Megiddo, Gezer, and Jericho[62]. Interestingly all these examples are also fronted by a cobra with a second being formed from the animals tail. They are all represented with hatched bodies.

---

[60] Tufnell 1958, pl.30:44; Giveon 1988, p.50/51 no.45; Petrie 1933, pl.iii:109.

[61] Tufnell 1958, pl.36:216; Guy 1938, pl.137:12.

[62] Briend/Humbert 1980, pl.88:6; Loud 1948, pl.151:119; Giveon 1985, 116 no.19; Kirkbride 1965, fig.291:13, fig.296:13 & fig.299:5.

This design is a more debased example of the naturalistic lion depicted on earlier scarabs which can be seen at sites such as Tell el-'Ajjul and in Nubia at Kerma and Aniba[63]. The way in which the carving of the design is executed suggests a later date: it is deeply cut out and then incised internally, similar to CN 14.

The *ḫpr* beetle is utilised in several of the Tomb 62 designs. The first type of design, showing the *ḫpr* beetle flanked by two cobras, has two examples (**CN 17, p.96/97, pl.IV & CN 18, p.96/97, pl.V**). The former has a badly depicted 'open' type head, plain back and simply represented legs, although a second incision at the rear of the scarab could represent a rear leg. The latter is a scaraboid (**CN 18**) with a human figure on the reverse. The base designs depict a *ḫpr* beetle flanked by two cobras with a badly drawn *nb* sign above (or below). The design is deeply cut out.

The *ḫpr* beetle flanked by cobras is once again a common design of the 'Hyksos' period with examples from Megiddo, Gibeon, Jericho, Lachish, Tell el-'Ajjul, Tell el-Dab'a, Kerma and Aniba. However, the design has two distinct categories. Firstly, as with the Pella design, the design can be placed horizontally along the length of the scarab base with the *ḫpr* beetle in the centre, flanked by cobras and occasionally placed upon a *nb* or *nwb* sign (see examples at Jericho, Tell el-'Ajjul, Gibeon, Kerma, Aniba and a seal impression on a jar handle from Tell el-Dab'a)[64]. Secondly, the design can be placed vertically down the length of the base with the beetle at the base and the cobras above with their tails hanging down (see examples at Megiddo and Lachish)[65].

---

[63] Petrie 1933, pl.iii:44; Reisner 1923, fig.168:76, fig.169:115; Steindorff 1937, pl.55:75.

[64] Kirkbride 1965, fig.300:31; Petrie 1931, pl.xiv:123, Petrie 1933, pl.iii:71, Petrie 1934, pl.v:137; Pritchard 1963, fig.70:10, Reisner 1923, fig.169:117; Steindorff 1937, pl.56:137; Milnar (pers. comm.).

[65] Loud 1948, pl.151:114; Tufnell 1958, pl.32:73.

The *ḫpr* beetle is again the centre of a design found on **CN 19 (p.98/99, pl.V)**. This scarab has an 'open' head type, plain back and triangular sides. The design comprises a *ḫpr* beetle surrounded by an interlocking spiral border.

Although the *ḫpr* beetle is a common design element, this particular design, i.e. in isolation with a simple scroll border, has its only 'close' parallels at three sites in Palestine, with none in Egypt and Nubia. Each site has different types of scroll border, with the exact parallel to the Pella design only found at Tell el–'Ajjul[66]. The design from Shechem illustrates a multi–interlocking spiral while that from Lachish has spirals with a looped end[67].

An unusual animal design found at Pella is that of a winged creature, **CN 20 (p.98/99, pl.V)**. It has a 'trapezoidal' type head, plain back and simply rendered legs. The design is set longitudinally down the length of the scarab with a cobra in front of the animal with a tree beneath and in between its back legs.

This design shares the deeply cut style exhibited in other animal designs, and obviously belongs to the same group chronologically. The winged creature is very rare, with no category assigned by Tufnell, and there is only one other example of such a design from Gezer[68]. It is possible that the Pella design, with its similar ambiguous head and stance is a bad imitation of it. Keel notes of such a creature: "Le griffon doit vraisemblablement sa présence sur les sceaux à sa signification de gardien et de protecteur" (Keel 1990, 183, n.83).

The final animal design scarab from Pella, **(CN 21, p.100/101, pl.V)**,

---

[66] Petrie 1931, pl.xiv:158; Petrie 1933, pl.iii:69.

[67] Horn 1962, fig.2:19; Tufnell 1958, pl.30:2.

[68] Macalister 1912, vol I, pl.lxiii:79.

has a 'trapezoidal' type head, plain back and simply represented legs which include a rear leg. The design consists of a Horus on a *nb* sign surrounded by four cobras. Though typical of the period and style in its content, it is a rare design with only two parallels from Tell el–'Ajjul[69]. The only differences lie in the drawing of the bird itself: the parallels from Tell el–'Ajjul have longer legs and pronounced beaks.

## 2.3 THE 'ANRA' SCARABS

There are five scarabs of the *ʿ–n–r* type at Pella, CN's 22, 23, 24, 25 & 26. They represent five very different types of styles of this design.

The first design, **CN 22 (p.100/101, pl.V)**, has a 'trapezoidal' head type, plain back and triangular legs. The design is the simplest one of the four, consisting of a central column of three vertical *nfr* signs flanked by the letters *ʿ–n–r–ʿ–ʿ* on the left and *ʿ–ʿ–n–r–ʿ–ʿ* on the right.

This type of design has many parallels, although only four very close ones, and they are all from Tell el–'Ajjul. Of the examples[70] only two have *nfr*'s running down the centre[71]. Other parallels are from further afield: there is one from Tell el–Yehudiyeh[72] although it is without the central *nfr* column; and a very close parallel from Syria,

---

[69]   Petrie 1931, pl.xiii: 29 & 59.

[70]   Petrie 1933, pl.iii:95; Petrie 1934, pl.v:69 & vii:210.

[71]   Petrie 1931, pl.xiv:155; Petrie 1952, pl.x:94.

[72]   Petrie 1906, pl.vi:4.

unfortunately without location, from the Hannover Museum[73]. There is also a parallel from the Basler Sammlungen collection in Switzerland[74], although this is again without the central *nfr* column.

The second design, **CN 23 (p.102/103, pl.VI)** is finely carved. It has a 'trapezoidal' head type, back decorated with a lotus flower and feathered legs. The design consists of a central cartouche encircling the letters ⸢-*r*-*n*-*r*-⸢. Above the cartouche is the papyrus plant of lower Egypt flanked by two *ḥ*⸢ signs. Below the cartouche lies a double papyrus which flanks a *ḥꜣst* above another *ḥ*⸢.

This scarab has no exact parallels. Scarabs from Tell el-'Ajjul, Egypt, and Aniba have the same cartouche, but different surrounding elements[75]. A scarab from Megiddo has no cartouche but the same filling papyri in the top panel area; another from Kerma[76] has the same combination of hieroglyphs over the whole base area.

The third type of design, **CN 24 (p.102/103, pl.VI)** has a 'lunate' type head with a plain back and triangular legs. The base design is an unusual combination of 'anra' with the (*nsw*) *bity* sign. *r*-*n*-⸢-*n*-*r* letters flank a central panel which consists of the *nsw*-*bity* sign (the *sw* is combined with the head of the bee and there are no *n*'s), with an ⸢*nḥ* sign below the head and a *nfr* below the *bity*. These both lie on their sides and above a large *nbw* sign.

There are only two other scarabs that combine 'anra' with the *nsw*-*bity*

[73]  Beste 1978, 1976:15.

[74]  Hornung & Staehelin 1976, 389 D2, pl.117.

[75]  Petrie 1934, pl.xi:433; Petrie 1925, pl.x:463; Steindorff 1937, pl.56:103.

[76]  Loud 1948, pl.149:50; Reisner 1923, pl.40/II-63.

28

sign. One is from Jericho and the other from Nubia, at Ukma (west)[77].

The fourth 'anra' scarab, **CN 25 (p.104/105, pl.VI)** has a 'trapezoidal' type head, plain back and simply represented legs. The base design seems initially to be a common 'anra' design. The hieroglyphs run down the length of the scarab ($r-\ulcorner-šn-n-\ulcorner-r$) surrounded by the 'panel' border. However, there are no similar borders as most have cross strokes in the middle sections, and the order of hieroglyphs are unusual and they also contain the *sn* sign.

Finally, the fifth type of design **(CN 26, p.104/105, pl.VI)** is distinguished by a large, central, rectangular, open ended, cartouche. This scarab has a 'trapezoidal' type head, plain back and triangular sides. The design comprises the central, rectangular cartouche surrounding the letters $htp-n-r-n-r$ running down the length of the cartouche. Above lies a $\ulcorner nh$ flanked by two *Hr* falcons standing on *nb* signs. The cartouche is flanked by $\ulcorner nh$ signs with possible squared off corners or sideways crowns of Upper Egypt.

The rectangular cartouche with 'anra' signs has examples at Megiddo, Jericho, and Tell el-Ajjul[78]. The latter design from Tell el-'Ajjul is the only one which supports a similar type of design above it i.e. *Hr* + *nfr* rather than $\ulcorner nh$. Those examples from Megiddo and Jericho have no filling ornament above, and have signs flanking the cartouche.

The 'anra' scarab has attracted attention from early this century and Weill was one of the first to reference this type (1910, 137). He associated the 'anra' combination with a King or Prince of this name, although this idea has never been received favourably.

---

[77] Kirkbride 1965, fig.287:9; Andreu 1987, 102/2.

[78] Loud 1948, pl.149:51; Kirkbride 1965, fig.286:12,13 & fig.285:16; Petrie 1934, pl.vii:168; Petrie 1952, pl.ix:63.

Petrie (1919, 46) initially proposed a reading of Du−ne−Ra, 'Gift of Ra' for this type of scarab therefore indicating an epithet rather than a name. However he later suggested a reading of 'ra−ne−ra' which he took as a blunder for the 'Ra−gave', a frequent type of theophoric name in the Middle Kingdom (Petrie 1925, 17), and later still indicated that it was perhaps copied from an Egyptian original, which may have been 'sa−re' − 'protection of Re' (Petrie 1930). Rowe (1936) accepted this former reading of 'ra−ne−ra' and suggested several variants.

Murray (1949) was the first who paid any detailed attention to the 'anra' scarab. Her conclusions were based on the fact that scarabs which exhibited such fine workmanship and material and were often set in gold, could and should not be so easily dismissed as 'nonsense hieroglyphs' (Murray 1949, 95). She argued that such skill and subsequent cost would not have been spent on ignorant copies of misunderstood inscriptions.

Murray believed that the inscriptions must have been important and relay some meaning to the wearers, and were in fact intended for the magical protection of the Royal 'name'. Due to associations with royal emblems it seemed probable that these scarabs were intended to commemorate 'the solemn ceremony of the giving of the Re−name to the King and to protect that name when given' (Murray 1949, 46).

Van Seters (1966, 64) only briefly referred to the 'anra' scarab but mentioned Murray's interpretation of their meaning. Niccacci's publication of two collections of scarabs from Jerusalem actually singles out the 'anra' scarab for special attention, and agrees with Murray, but believes that these scarabs were not used as seals but as amulets, due to their magical power ordained through the possession of the name (Niccacci 1980, 30).

In Hornung and Staehelin's publication of the Basler collection of scarabs (1976, 51) the interpretation of the scarabs still poses difficulties. They suggest either a connection with the name of the sun god Re', when the inscriptions are presented in their full, unshortened form, or possible associations with one of the *abracadabra* magical words that exist in later Egyptian magical texts.

They, like Ward (1987, 526), also follow Stock's suggestion (1942, 24) that the 'anra' scarabs could have originated in the *Neferzeichen* patterns of the Middle Kingdom. Ward concludes from this that the symbols should at least make some sense in Egyptian (1987, 526 n.77).

Tufnell ascribes these scarabs to her class 3C or formulae scarabs. She notes that they are neatly cut and arranged and that the designers of the formulae were well acquainted with Egyptian hieroglyphic motifs although they appear only to make limited sense (Tufnell 1984, 121).In Giveon's publication of some material in the British Museum, he finds that the 'combinations are meaningless, although pleasing to the eye' (1985, 18).

The 'anra' scarab warrants a serious in-depth investigation chronologically and epigraphically. Ward (1987) raised some serious questions regarding its interpretation, for it seems that this scarab type may not only yield valuable evidence for the comparative chronology of the MBIIB–C/SIP, but also for the nature of the 'Hyksos' relations between Egypt and Palestine at that time.

Preliminary investigations have indicated that seventy–five percent of the scarabs are associated in some way with signs representing 'royalty' i.e. crowns (of Lower Egypt), cartouches or the 'royal' panel design of the 'Hyksos'. Equally, the sign conceptualising 'peace' is also frequent.

Three hundred scarabs of this type have been identified from Nubia, Egypt, Palestine and Syria. There is a common assumption that they are characteristic of the SIP because they did not appear in quantity in Egyptian deposits until the SIP, and that they originated in Palestine as they are more numerous during the SIP in that location[79].

However, recent excavations from Memphis, Egypt, have brought to light two 'anra' seal impressions[80]. These are of the utmost importance, as the deposits to which they belong are clearly contexted and date from the mid to late XIIth Dynasty. This provides clear evidence that the origin of the $^c-n-r$ scarab was earlier than hitherto suggested.

## 2.4 PATTERNED SCARABS

### 2.4.i Cross Pattern

There are two scarabs CN 27 and 28, which belong to Tufnell's 'cross pattern' class (1984, 125). **CN 27 (p.106/107, pl.VII)** has an 'open' head type, plain back and triangular legs. **CN 28 (p.106/107, pl.VII)** has a 'trapezoidal' head type, plain back and triangular legs. The latter has the more common 'cross pattern' design of the two, with examples from Megiddo, Jericho, Lachish, Tell el-'Ajjul, Beth Pelet, Tell el Yehudiyeh and Tell el-Dab'a[81]. There is only one other example of CN 27 at Beth Pelet[82].

---

[79]   Ward 1987, 526; Niccacci 1980, 25.

[80]   My thanks to Mr D.G. Jeffereys, Director of the Memphis Excavations and to the Egypt Exploration Society for their kind permission to use the sealing evidence.

[81]   Loud 1948, pl.150:63, pl.152:163, Guy 1938, pl.105:6; Kirkbride 1965, fig.292:3; fig.286:1; fig.283:2; Tufnell 1958, pl.32:111,112; pl.34:168; Petrie 1934, pl.vii:184; Petrie 1952, pl.x:147; Petrie 1930, pl.vii:14; Petrie 1906, pl.ix:139, Mlinar (unpublished) 510.

[82]   Petrie 1930, pl.vii:41.

## 2.4.ii  Concentric Circles

There is one example of this type of scarab at Pella, **CN 29 (p.108/109, pl.VII)**. It has a lunate type head, plain back and simply represented legs. The base design consists of four concentric circles, with a drilled hole in the centre joined together by a meandering curvilinear line.

Concentric circles are known from the FIP where they were very popular, and they continued to be made throughout the Middle Kingdom and SIP (Tufnell 1984, 124). They would also seem to be an intensely popular design during this latter period as they can be found in Syria (Byblos), throughout Palestine (Tell Keisan, Shechem, Tel Aviv, Megiddo, Gezer, Gibeon, Jericho, Lachish, Tell el–'Ajjul, Tel Jemmeh, Beth Pelet), in Egypt (Tell el–Dab'a, Tell el–Yehudiyeh, Gurob, Haragah, Masmas) and Nubia (Uronarti, Kerma).

However, from the many examples found at all these sites, there is no pattern exactly the same as the design found at Pella. The closest design is found at Tell el–Dab'a in Egypt[83], unfortunately from a secondary context with no date.

## 2.4.iii  Interwoven Design

The two scarabs with this design, CN 30 and 31 are examples of another popular pattern of the SIP. **CN 30 (p.108/109, pl.VII)** has a badly engraved 'trapezoidal' type head, plain back and simply represented legs. **CN 31 (p.110/111, pl.VIII)** is a scaraboid with no features, although its side has a series of small incisions akin to 'feathering'. Both scarabs have the same base design of a 'central twist' which is connected above, below and to, side incisions.

---

[83]  Mlinar (unpublished), no.1031.

There are variations (Tufnell 1984, 125) of this pattern, but the type that occurs at Pella can also be found at Megiddo, Lachish, Tell Beit Mirsim, Beth Pelet, and is very popular at Tell el-'Ajjul[84].

The design is also found at Kerma[85]. Perhaps an early version of this design i.e. with the central twist but not joined above and below, is found at Tell el-Yehudiyeh[86], Tell el-Dab'a[87], Gurob[88] and also at Gezer[89] and Jericho[90]. There are only two examples of this type of design surrounded by a border as CN 31 at Beth Pelet[91] and Lachish[92].

---

[84] Loud 1948, pl.149:27; Tufnell 1958, pl.30:32, pl.30:61 pl.34:194; Albright 1938, pl.28:12; Petrie 1930, pl.xii:122, pl.xxii:215; Starkey/Harding 1932, pl.xliv:71; Petrie 1931, pl.xiii:17, pl.xiv:177; Petrie 1932, pl.vii:1, pl.viii:160; Petrie 1933, pl.iv:131; Petrie 1934 pl.v:51, pl.vii:249, 266, pl.ix:280; Petrie 1952, pl.x:158–162.

[85] Reisner 1923, pl.40/II–61.

[86] Petrie 1906, pl.viii:46.

[87] Mlinar (unpublished) no.903.

[88] Brunton/Engelhart 1927, pl.xl:7.

[89] Giveon 1985, 122 no.37.

[90] Kirkbride 1965, fig.296:2.

[91] Starkey/Harding 1932, pl.xliv:71.

[92] Tufnell 1958, pl.30:61.

## 2.5 HIEROGLYPH DESIGNS

These can be most easily split into simple and more complicated patterns. To the former group belong CN 33–40, and to the latter, CN 41–45. Exact or 'close' parallels to these designs are rare, and so aspects of the designs are also considered.

Tufnell divides this class of Egyptian signs and symbols by the most frequent and significant symbols. There is, therefore, no specific class exists for **CN 33 (p.112/113, pl.VIII)** and **CN 37 (p.116/117, pl.IX)**. The former has a triangular 'trapezoidal' head, a plain back and simply depicted legs. The base design consists of a spiral flanked by two wilting papyri. The latter has a 'trapezoidal' type head, plain back and simply depicted legs. The design consists of a $wd_3t$-sign above an $^cnh$ within a cartouche, flanked by standing and wilting papyri.

There is only one exact parallel for the more simple scroll and papyrus design. This is found at Megiddo[93]. There are three other examples of a scroll surrounded by a double papyrus (standing and wilting) at Lachish and Tell el-'Ajjul[94]. There are no parallels for the $wd_3t$ eye and $^cnh$ within a cartouche occurring together.

**CN 34 (p.112/113, pl.VIII)** has an 'open' head type, plain back and simply represented legs. The base design consists of a simple pattern of three $šn$ signs above a $nb$ sign with an inverted lotus flower with five petals above. There is only one exact parallel for this design at Tell el-Ajjul[95]. Three $šn$ signs together in the mid panel are also

---

[93]   Loud 1948, pl.150:88.

[94]   Tufnell 1958, pl.34:156; Petrie 1932, pl.viii:152; Petrie 1934 pl.xi:412.

[95]   Petrie 1931, pl.xiii:5.

found at Megiddo, Gezer, Jericho, Tell el–Dab'a and Aniba[96]. Although the motifs above and below differ, an *nb* sign is almost always included.

**CN 35 (p.114/115, pl.IX)** has the triangular 'trapezoidal' head, a plain back and simply represented sides. The base design consists of a central panel of two *ʿnḫ*'s flanking a *nfr* with a small *nb* sign below and a double papyri above. **CN 42 (p.120/121, pl.X)** is a scaraboid with notching around the sides. It has a detailed base design consisting of groups of *ʿnḫ*'s flanking *nfr*'s and vice versa, flanked in turn by two crowns of Upper/Lower Egypt, all on a *nb* sign. Parallels can be drawn for the *ʿnḫ* flanking the *nfr* sign, and they are found at Tell el–'Ajjul, Lahun and Uronarti[97].

**CN 36 (p.114/115, pl.IX)** has an 'open' head type, plain back and triangular legs. The base design consists of an interlocking scroll design with a papyrus scroll above. At first this seems to be a common scroll pattern. On further investigation however, only four examples of this type of pattern occur outside of Pella with none from Palestine – at Tell el–Dab'a, Tell el–Yehudiyeh, Kahun and Kerma[98].

Other examples of this pattern occur at Sidon, Megiddo, Gibeon, Jericho, Tell el–'Ajjul and Beth Pelet with further examples from Kahun[99]. All these examples include double scroll patterns, rather

---

[96] Loud 1948, pl.150:58; Macalister 1912, pl.ccix:25; Kirkbride 1965, fig.285:10; Mlinar (unpublished) no.621; Steindorff 1937, pl.55:90.

[97] Petrie 1952, pl.ix:85; Petrie/Brunton/Murray 1923, pl.lxiv:274; Reisner 1955, fig.12:288–299.

[98] Mlinar (unpublished) no.1035; Petrie 1906, pl.ix:127; Petrie 1891, pl.x:155,157; Reisner 1923, fig.168:40.

[99] Tufnell 1975/6, fig.1:11, Loud 1948, pl.150:75; Pritchard 1963, fig.71:8; Kirkbride 1965, fig.291:3; Petrie 1932, pl.viii:122; Petrie 1930, pl.vii:45; Petrie 1891, pl.x:154–158.

than the above examples which only contain one single pattern.

**CN 38 (p.116/117, pl.IX)** has a base design depicting a *nbw* sign surrounded by a hooked, oblong scrolled border. It has a 'trapezoidal' head, plain back and simple, feathered legs. There is only one other design such as this, from Gezer[100].

**CN 39 (p.118/119, pl.IX)** has a 'lunate' head, with a plain back and very simply represented legs. The base design consists of two pairs of oblong, hooked scrolls enclosing an unidentified sign. The 'puggle' or 'two pairs, oblong, hooked, scroll border' (Tufnell 1984, 128) is a dominant pattern at Jericho and occurs with less frequency at Shechem, Megiddo and Gezer, and there is one example from Tell el-Yehudiyeh[101]. All examples have varying internal hieroglyphs.

**CN 40 (p.118/119, pl.X)** has an 'open' type head, plain back and simply represented legs. The base design consists a central $wd_3t$-sign flanked by a standing and wilting papyri. There are no parallels for this design.

**CN 41 (p.120/121, pl.X)** has a lunate head, plain back and triangular legs. Its base design consists of 4 panels of hieroglyphs running down the length of the base. The top panel has a $w_3d$ sign flanked by *Horus* falcons, then double $wd_3t$ eyes, underneath a *ḫpr* beetle flanked by *ʿnḫ* signs within cartouches all on top of a *nbw* sign. All the hieroglyphs used are popular during the SIP and so there is no exact parallel although different combinations of the different symbols are

---

[100] Macalistar 1912, pl.ccix:8.

[101] Kirkbride 1965, fig.282:15; fig.289:15; fig.303:12; fig.295:12; fig.300:1; fig.302:1,14,16; fig.296:3; fig.288:4; fig.299:13; Horn 1962, fig.2:22; Loud 1948, pl.149:22,26,47, Guy 1938, pl.105:11; Macalister 1912, pl.ccvi:19; Petrie 1906, pl.ix:131.

found in Palestine, Egypt and Nubia[102].

**CN 43 (p.122/123, pl.X)** has a 'trapezoidal' type head, a plain back and feathered legs. The base design consists of an assortment of hieroglyphs arranged randomly. **CN 45 (p.124/125. pl.XI)** has a lunate head, plain back and feathered legs. The base design consists of randomly spaced hieroglyphs surrounded by an interlocking scroll border[103].

Both these scarabs are without exact parallels. The hieroglyphs are placed at random which is only repeated on approximately ten other scarabs from Tell el–Dab'a, Ugarit, Tell Aviv, Jericho, Tell el–'Ajjul and Beth Pelet[104]. CN 45 also places the hieroglyphs not only at random but also upside down. The scroll border surrounding these hieroglyphs is found at Beth Shan, Gezer and Jericho[105].

There are no close parallels for **CN 44 (p.122/123, pl.X)**, comprising a double $^cnh$ flanked by *uraei*, then a $k_3$ flanked by *Ḥr*–falcons on top of a *nfr* flanked by $^cnh$ and $w_3d$'s on top of a *nb* sign. If the flanking *uraei* and falcons are taken as royal or decorative elements, and the *nb* as the common base ornament, then the central vertical line reads

---

[102] E.g. At Aphek (Giveon 1988, p.56/7 no.55) are the $wd_3t$ eyes and the *ḫpr* placed in the middle but different filling elements; Tell Jerishe (Giveon 1988, p.64/5 no.65) and Aniba (Steindorff 1937, pl.56:128) have the $^cnh$ sign within the circles; Tell el–Dab'a again uses the double $wd_3t$ eye (Mlinar (unpublished), no.108); Megiddo has an example of the $wd_3t$ eyes, *ḫpr* and $^cnh$'s but not within the circles (Rowe 1936, no.3) and Jericho (Kirkbride 1965, fig.295:17) has examples of the $^cnh$'s within circles and a *nbw* at the bottom.

[103] Both these scarabs could be considered as cryptograms (see Schulman 1975, 1978) a concept under investigation.

[104] Mlinar (unpublished) no.1006; Schaeffer 1939, pl.v:11,14; Kaplan 1955, fig.6:17; Kirkbride 1965, fig.284:3; fig.300:19; fig.302:7; fig.298:19; Petrie 1931, pl.xiii:23; Petrie 1930, pl.x:97.

[105] Rowe 1936, pl.iv:143; Macalister 1912, pl.ccvi:24; Kirkbride 1965, fig.291:11.

$k_3 - nfr - r^c$.

## 2.6    NB.TY AND PLANT DESIGN

This design was popular in the FIP and takes its name from the initial composition of the design which consisted of two *nb* signs joined by a horizontal line, which then formed the base line for various symbols. From the XIIth Dynasty onwards the true *nb.ty* design is replaced by several variations on this theme. Ward (1978, 68) comments on the use of the single spiral in the central place flanked by red crowns which is later replaced by double papyri flanked by a full S spiral or one or more *šn* signs.

The three Pella examples, CN 46, 47, 48 all consist of the basic two sn signs flanked by a standing and wilting papyri. An *nb* sign lies above the *šn* signs and the three only differ on the make up of the base line. **CN 46 (p.124/125, pl.XI)** is a scaraboid and has no other features besides the base design, which differs from its counterpart because it has diagonal vertical lines below the base line and is surrounded by a border. Both **CN 47 (p.126/127, pl.XI)** and **CN 48 (p.126/127, pl.XI)** have triangular 'trapezoidal' heads, plain backs and simply depicted legs. The former design has two *nb* signs with horizontal vertical lines in between below the base line. The latter base design has a series of small horizontal lines below its base line.

Tufnell notes that 'the scarcity of the design and its variants at all sites...emphasises the fact that it hardly survives into the Twelfth Dynasty, either in Egypt or Tell el-'Ajjul' (Tufnell 1984, 118).

This is surprising as there are examples of this type of design from Egypt, Syria, Palestine, Egypt and Nubia dating to the SIP. There is an elaborate design from an early strata at Tell el-Dab'a (stratum G; no.9) as well as a later more corrupt design, although with stylised red crowns, from a later stratum (stratum D3:711) and Tell el–Yehudiyeh has one example. It has the original *nb* signs as a bottom line with the later double papyri, which flank a single *ʿnḫ* sign[106]. Other examples from Egypt and Nubia are from Kahun, Harageh and Masmas[107].

In Nubia there are a number of examples from Uronarti[108] although none of these have a *šn* sign in the mid area, and there are two examples from Kerma[109], of which the latter is a direct parallel of CN 48.

Examples from Syria come from Byblos and Sidon[110]. The Byblos scarabs have the original *nb* base line with one *šn* sign; the parallel from Sidon is a true later rendition with double papyri, two *šn* in the middle but on a base line of two *nb* signs.

From Palestine, there are parallels from two sites, Tell el–'Ajjul and Gezer. There are ten examples from Tell el–'Ajjul, with diverse mid panels and base lines, but all with the standing and wilting papyri [111]. One Gezer example has two signs for the mid section, which is quite unusual, while another supports three *šn* signs and an unusual

---

[106]  Griffith 1890, pl.ix:136.

[107]  Petrie/Brunton/Murray 1923, pl.lxv:314; Petrie 1890, pl.x:47; Petrie 1891, pl.x:113; Englebach/Grunn 1923, pl.xx:63,65,66; Emery/Kirwan 1935, pl.32:78.

[108]  Reisner 1955, fig.12:304–308, 348.

[109]  Reisner 1923, pl.40/II-60 & pl.40/II-62.

[110]  Dunand 1937, pl.cxxx:1388, 1405; pl.cxxxv:2709; Tufnell 1975/6, fig.1:5.

[111]  Petrie 1934, pl.v:88, pl. vii:152, pl.vii:248, pl.ix:314; Petrie 1952, pl. xi:103–105.

base line[112].

Ward noted that the double papyrus plant motif appeared more often in the Middle Kingdom and SIP and was generally 'more at home in the XIIth – XVth Dynasties' (1978, 72). The above examples would clearly fall into this range and would indicate that the design continues for a longer period than initially thought by Tufnell.

## 3.    SUMMARY

The group of scarabs from Tomb 62 are noteworthy because they are one of the largest, well contexted groups of scarabs found in the southern Levant. Much is known of western and southern Palestine, but this group of archaeological material adds new evidence and raises anew questions regarding the cultural and political position of the Southern Levant during the SIP/MBIIB/C Periods.

## 3.1    DESIGNS

The distribution patterns of typologically similar scarabs is worth noting and two main points emerge. Firstly, Tell el–'Ajjul stands out as the main site associated with the Pella scarabs, as over seventy five percent of the scarabs have parallels from that site.

Secondly, there is a high proportion of sites with parallels to the scarabs from Tomb 62 which are located outside of Palestine. i.e. often the only parallel or similar design to Pella will be found in Egypt (often Tell el–Dab'a or Tell el–Yehudiyeh) or Nubia (e.g. 'anra'

---

[112] Macalister 1912, pl.cciia:2, pl.cciiia:2.

41

cartouche design, 'anra' centrally divided design, 'anra' *nsw–bity* design, interwoven design, hieroglyph designs and the *nb.ty* design).

Within the recognisable style of designs executed during the above period, the Pella scarabs stand out. With several unique design concepts and a style of seal engraving that is noticeably different to its contemporaries, although still recognisable as belonging within the general parameters of the period, this leads to the suggestion that the scarabs could have been manufactured in the area. As Pella is a site of regional significance, it would not be unreasonable to suggest the scarabs were manufactured at the site. It is difficult to point to any single features that could be ascertained as a "hallmark" of the Pella workshop, it is rather the execution of the design that seems distinctive.

## 3.2   MATERIAL

From the tests completed, it would seem that the main material used for the manufacture of the Pella scarabs was the naturally occurring soap stone, steatite. What is less clear is the origin of the steatite so employed[113].

It is probable that the amethyst was imported to the site, as it does not occur naturally around Pella, unlike the wood which could have come from the surrounding region. It is possible that the faience scarabs could have been manufactured there as well. Faience was

---

[113] Steatite does not occur naturally in Palestine/Jordan. It is found in small deposits in the mountains of southern Syria and in large quantities in Cyprus and the eastern deserts of Egypt. (My thanks to Dr. John Powell of the British Geological Survey for this information).

manufactured in Palestine during the MBIIB/C period[114], and the crudeness of the faience scarabs could indicate that such a process was taking place at the site itself.

## 3.3   CONCLUSIONS

The MBIIB/C in Palestine, corresponding to the SIP in Egypt, is a dynamic period because there is, as yet, no satisfactory political or cultural synthesis. The appropriate level of interaction between Palestine and Egypt remains unclear, as does the situation within Palestine itself.

An analysis of the scarab evidence from Pella cannot be expected to provide comprehensive answers to the problems of this period, but they do represent one strand of what must be a multi-disciplinary investigation if the problems are ever to be addressed adequately.

Two sites identified of major significance to any understanding of the Hyksos SIP are Tell el-Dab'a (Avaris) and Tell el-'Ajjul (Sharuhen)[115]. The primary association of the Pella scarab corpus is with Tell el-'Ajjul and not with those sites geographically contiguous. Together with the royal-name scarab evidence this suggests a special

---

[114] See Sagona 1980, and personal communication with Dr E.J. Peltenburg, December 1990.

[115] The identification of Tell el-'Ajjul as Sharuhen is still debated: Albright (1929,7) originally proposed the site of Tell el-Farah (Beth Pelet) which was accepted by Avi-Yonah/Stern (1975, 1074); Bimson (1981, 243-244) and Beitzel (1985, 63). Kempinski (1974, 245-152) suggested Tell el-'Ajjul and has been supported by Stewart (1974) and Weinstein (1981, 241), although still disputed (Hoffmeier 1989,184; Weinstein 1991, 106; Hoffmeier 1991).

and hitherto undetected relationship between Pella and Tell el-'Ajjul. Whether this material cultural association has any greater political expression cannot, as yet, be determined.

# APPENDIX A

Appendix A:  The Pella scarabs and Ward & Tufnell's typology

# APPENDIX A

## TYPOLOGY

For comparative purposes, Ward and Tufnell's typology is used and expanded to accommodate the Pella scarabs. Although the percentage tables are interesting, they do not indicate the amount of diversification amongst designs within a group, and so will not be used here. (See Table 1 for a correlation of the Pella scarabs with Ward and Tufnell's classification).

## HEAD TYPES

Tufnell proposes four head types: A: Lunate, B: Open, C: Square, D: Trapezoidal. Six new sub-categories need to be added within the major Classes.

Firstly, among Class A: Lunate, group 6, a new sub-division (i) can be added to account for the types found at Pella which do not join the head as illustrated within Fig.12 (Tufnell 1984, 32), but obviously belong to the same group.

There are a number of scarabs at Pella that exhibit a more 'triangular' shaped head. The types appearing at Pella can be accommodated by adding a subclass to Class B, group 2 – for those which are enclosed with an 'hour-glass' outline, and the rest are an extension of Class D, group 8.

Finally, within Class D, four new sub-divisions are necessary. Firstly, in group 3 and group 5 a sub-division is needed to account for those heads without baselines. Secondly, in group 4, a sub-division is needed to account for the trapezoidal head type which has additional markings and finally, as mentioned above, within group 8, there should be a further category to distinguish these triangular head types with eyes, as they are a frequent division at Pella[1].

## LEG TYPES

Three new categories need to be established. The first can be slotted into section 'd3' currently left free. It represents plain, triangular legs, but also with a plain, diagonal back leg represented. A sub–division of class 'e2' and 'e11' needs to be established for those types of legs which also have feathering.

## BASE DESIGN

Tufnell has divided the base designs into eleven classes.

Class 1 accounts for "liner patterns", and a sub–division has been added to section B, to cater for those geometric patterns which are symmetrical.

Class 3 deals with hieroglyph design, which are classified according to those signs which occur most frequently and which, according to Tufnell, are the most significant. Therefore, many of the hieroglyph designs from Pella would fall into class 3A, 'varia', as they do not exhibit those signs which have been deemed 'frequent or significant'.

A new sub–division could at least move three of the scarabs from this general class. CN 33, 37, 40 all have flanking papyri, either double or single variety. This could be a sub–division of class 3B8: (i): single flanking papyri, and (ii): double flanking papyri.

---

[1]   I wish to note here that certain headtypes classified as Class D8 and which have been included by me as Class D8(i), are not, I believe, strictly speaking a type of head. The 'triangular' head type illustrated here is actually an elongated clypeus, often represented with eyes: but I have followed the typology in order to establish a sense of continuity.

Of the animal designs, Class 9, there is only one scarab from Pella that does not fit within the types offered by Tufnell. This is the 'winged creature', CN 20. This can easily be included by the establishment of a new group, 9H.

The figured scarabs, Class 10, are slightly harder to fit within the parameters of Tufnell's typology. Tufnell has divided the categories of human figures into four Groups: A: standing, B: two or more figures, standing and/or kneeling; C: kneeling and D: goddesses. In turn they are further categorised by their type of head; 1: human, 2: mythological/ zoomorphic; and finally by the emblems they carry.

Four of the six figured scarabs cannot be categorised within the current typology. Firstly, within class A, provision needs to be made for a figure with raised arms, such as CN 10. This can be added as a sub–section 'g'.

Secondly, within Class B, there needs to be account taken of one or both figures which may be *seated*, as Pella CN 11. This is harder to fit within Tufnell's sequence, but could be provided for with a sub–division after the class. i.e. Class B, sub–class (i): seated figure, then the type of head etc. This type of division can then be extended to include Pella CN 6, which shows double figures neither standing, kneeling or seated. This is sub–class (ii).

Finally a new group needs to be added to Class D, that of goddesses, following the recent work of Winter (1983) and Schroer (1989). They have successfully demonstrated that there is a difference between the frontal standing figure, arms hanging by sides, head facing front; and that figure with the same stance, but with its head facing to the side. The former is generally acknowledged to represent the Egyptian 'Hathor' goddess, while the latter has been shown to have a Syrian origin (Schroer 1989, 93–5) (see section 2.2.i).

# ROYAL NAME SCARABS

Outside Egypt, Apophis is known only by his scarabs. There are only four examples and they are all found at Tell el–'Ajjul (Weinstein 1979, fig. 2). There is sufficient information to compare three of these scarabs with the one excavated at Pella. The first (Petrie 1931, pl.xiii:2; Tufnell 1984, no. 3437) has an open type head, with simply rendered legs indicated by a single incised line and a back which has the prothorax and elytra divided, and then the elytra again divided into two, by single incised lines. The second scarab (Petrie 1931, pl.xiv:143; Tufnell, 1984, no.3436) also has an open head, simply rendered legs but the more typical plain back. The final scarab (Petrie 1932, pl.7:77; Tufnell 1984, no.3434) has an open head, plain back and simply depicted legs.

These features generally agree with Ward's sequence (discussed in more detail below), with only the late back type of the first example standing out of the sequence, as does the Pella example.

It is worth comparing the results of Ward's work on the Royal Name scarabs from *Studies on Scarab Seals II*, with the Pella examples. Ward has provided an interesting sequence of the 'Hyksos' kings based on stylistic analysis of all scarab features ie. backs, sides, heads and leg types. However, he makes one assumption, which not everyone will concede: that the XVIth Dynasty does not exist, because 'historical studies have suffered from attempts to account for Manetho's XVIth Dynasty which never, in fact, existed' (Ward 1984, 162). Thus the XIIIth, XVth and XVIIIth dynasties follow each other chronologically.

To establish his sequence he works backwards from Khamudy. This is the name given in the Turin Canon for the sixth and final ruler of the group of six 'rulers of foreign countries', to whom he assigns 108 years of combined rule. Khamudy is the sole name preserved of this group.

Ward identifies Auserre Apophis as the 5th King on the Turin list

(Ward 1984, 162); but there is less certainty and agreement about the determination of the other four. Ward suggests Seuserenre Khyan and Maybre Sheshi are generally accepted as two other candidates, but there is little agreement of the remaining two. Hayes favours Yakubher and a second Apophis; Helck proposes Semqen and Anather, Von Beckerath, Yakubher and Sekhaenre and Bietak, Yakubher and Sharek (Ward 1984, 162 n.73).

However, Ward believes that a general scarab style is associated with a group of royal names which are characteristic of the XVth dynasty, and more importantly, a definite chronology of stylistic development exists within this general scarab style. Firstly, he defines four 'more or less' homogeneous stages of scarab style that can be identified on the basis of several details used in their manufacture.

The rulers included in Ward's four stages are:

| | | |
|---|---|---|
| 1. | Seuserenre Khyan | |
| | Meruserre Yakubher | |
| 2. | Mayebre Sheshi | |
| | Khauserre | |
| | Amu | |
| 3. | Nubuserrre | |
| | Sekhanre | |
| | Ahetepre | |
| 4. | Auserre Apophis | |

Taking these four groups, he concludes with regard to scarab length, that Apophis scarabs have a small average length of 13–18mm and that there is a general decrease in size towards the end of the SIP. The Pella example fits the end of this size range, measuring 18mm.

Ninety–five percent of Hyksos scarabs have plain backs. Therefore any decorated backs are quite distinctive. Ward finds that the only decorated backs he has seen occur early in his sequence, associated with Khyan, Yakubher and Sheshi, and he thus believes them to be chronologically related. If this is correct, then the Pella example is therefore exceptional as no other parallels exist.

Legs are generally defined by Ward as chip carved (types 'd5' & 'd6'), although the scored simple type ('e11') is also common among the Apophis scarabs. The Pella example fits with this aspect of Ward's sequence, as it has simply scored legs.

The Pella scarab of Auserre Apophis can be summarised as follows: the *nsw – bity* name is written within a cartouche and has an appropriate epithet. Although at the larger end of the scale for a scarab at the end of Ward's sequence on size, the scarab is still within his set 'limits' for this type, and the same applies to its leg type. The only real difference is the decorated back which seems to be very unusual according to Ward's sequence, but does not necessary question an Egyptian manufacture.

Regarding the Nubuserre scarab, Ward notes that the 'open' type of head is unusual for scarabs of his third group of SIP kings in which he has placed Nubuserre. He finds that the average length is 16–19mm, into which the Pella scarab falls, and that all these scarabs exhibit simply constructed legs except for a couple of examples. The panel design is also common in Nubuserre's scarabs.

## CONCLUSIONS

## DIMENSIONS

Ward discussed the importance of dimensions and studied several factors relating to size, but found that they produced no meaningful results except for the length of the scarab which Ward found to be 'a significant general clue to dating' (Ward 1978, 20). Tufnell found that the largest scarabs are found in the XIIIth Dynasty and thereafter the scarabs decreased in size (Tufnell 1984, 28).

The most popular length within Tomb 62 was the 17–23mm range which accounted for 55% of the scarabs, although the 11–16mm range also accounted for 42% Both chamber 1 and 2 had a dominant length of 23mm (i.e. Chamber 1: 30% = 17–23mm; 19% = 11–16; Chamber 2: 24% = 17–23mm; 20% = 11–16mm). This suggests that both chambers are contemporary. Chamber 3 had two scarabs measuring 19 x 13mm, which also corresponds with chambers 1 and 2.

## HEAD, BACK AND SIDES

The most popular head types of the Pella scarabs are types 'D' and 'B', Trapezoidal and Open. According to Tufnell's data, this then corresponds most closely to Jericho groups III–V and 'Ajjul, groups III–II.

The most common side type at Pella is undoubtedly side 'e11', the simple, scored legs, which is generally recognised as epitomising the 'Hyksos' period in Egypt. E11 is common in Jericho, group V and 'Ajjul, groups III and II. The second most common side at Pella was the new class, 'd3', of triangularly depicted legs which include the back leg.

The plain back type is undoubtedly the most common of the SIP, and this is reflected at Pella. Pella has a small number of decorated backs which is less usual for this time.

There is no doubt that the scarabs found within Tomb 62 correspond generally to the "trends" established by Ward and Tufnell, with the new categories emphasising the individuality of the site.

An attempt was made to distinguish geographically in Palestine, from North to South, any established trends within the head, back and side types between the scarabs from Tomb 62 and their parallels.

None emerged within the head and back types, as the 'trapezoidal' heads and the 'plain' backs dominated these categories. However, within the leg types, it was superficially possible to ascertain a trend towards more realistic representation in the South; although this needs further investigation before it can be established with certainty.

Table 1: Correlation of Pella scarabs with Ward and Tufnell's typology

| C.N. | DIMENSIONS (cm) | HEAD | BACK | SIDE | DESIGN |
|------|-----------------|------|------|------|--------|
| 1 | 1.95 x 1.35 x 0.85 | *A6i | O | *d3 | 11A |
| 2 | 1.9 x 1.3 x 0.85 | – | O | e11 | 11A |
| 3 | 1.5 x 1.0 x 0.75 | A4 | O | d13 | 11A |
| 4 | 1.6 x 1.15 x 0.8 | *D8i | O | e11 | *10D3 |
| 5 | 1.75 x 1.15 x 0.7 | – | O | e11 | *10D3 |
| 6 | 2.1 x 1.4 x 0.95 | *D4i | O | e11 | *10Bi3f |
| 7 | 2.0 x 1.35 x 0.85 | *D8i | O | e11 | 10A1a |
| 8 | 1.5 x 1.05 x 0.65 | *D8i | O | e11 | 10C1a |
| 9 | 1.6 x 1.1 x 0.55 | D8 | O | e11 | 10C1a |
| 10 | 2.0 x 1.45 x 0.95 | – | O | *d3 | *10A1g |
| 11 | 2.6 x 1.9 x 1.0 | D5 | dec | *d3 | *10Bii1 |
| 12 | 1.7 x 1.2 x 0.8 | – | O | e11 | 9B |
| 13 | 1.5 x 1.05 x 0.7 | – | O | e11 | 9B |
| 14 | 1.85 x 0.8 x 0.75 | *B2i | I | *d3 | 9B |
| 15 | 2.05 x 1.4 x 0.85 | D1 | O | *d3 | 9E |
| 16 | 2.0 x 1.45 x 0.9 | *D3i | O | e11 | 9E |
| 17 | 1.6 x 1.15 x 0.65 | B4 | O | e2 | 9C1 |
| 18 | 2.3 x 1.5 x 0.85 | – | – | e11 | 10A3c/9C1 |
| 19 | 1.65 x 1.15 x 0.8 | B2 | O | *d3 | 7B1iib |
| 20 | 1.9 c 1.35 x 0.85 | D5 | O | e11 | *9H |
| 21 | 1.7 x 1.2 x 0.8 | D5 | O | *d3 | 9C3 |
| 22 | 1.75 x 1.2 x 0.75 | *D3i | O | *d3 | 3C |

* new category

Table 1: continued

| C.N. | DIMENSIONS (cm) | HEAD | BACK | SIDE | DESIGN |
|------|-----------------|------|------|------|--------|
| 23 | 1.3 x  2.0 x 0.9 | D3 | dec | e9 | 3C |
| 24 | 1.7 x 1.2 x 0.9 | A6 | O | d4 | 3C |
| 25 | 1.9 x 1.3 x 0.85 | *D5i | O | e11 | *9H |
| 26 | 2.6 x 1.8 x 1.15 | D5 | O | *d3 | 3C |
| 27 | 1.9 x 1.4 x 0.85 | B4 | O | *d3 | 5 |
| 28 | 1.9 x 1.4 x 0.9 | D5 | O | *d3 | 5 |
| 29 | 1.3 x 0.9 x 0.6 | A5 | O | e11 | 4C1 |
| 30 | 1.45 x 1.0 x 0.65 | D1 | O | e11 | 6C2 |
| 31 | 2.35 x 1.6 x 0.85 | – | O | e11 | 6C2 |
| 32 | 2.1 x 1.4 x 0.65 | – | dec | e11 | 1B1 |
| 33 | 1.5 x 1.0 x 0.65 | *D8i | O | e11 | *3B8i |
| 34 | 1.5 x 1.1 x 0.6 | *B2i | O | e11 | 3A3 |
| 35 | 1.45 x 1.0 x 0.65 | *D8i | O | e2 | 3A3 |
| 36 | 1.65 x 1.2 x 0.75 | *B2i | O | e5 | 2B2 |
| 37 | 1.5 x 1.0 x 0.7 | C7 | O | e2 | *3B8ii |
| 38 | 1.65 x 1.15 x 0.75 | D6 | O | *e2i | 3B6/7A2a |
| 39 | 1.35 x 0.95 x 0.7 | – | O | *e11i | 7B2iia |
| 40 | 1.2 x 0.8 x 0.6 | B2 | O | e11 | *3B8ii |
| 41 | 1.9 x 1.2 x 0.7 | A6 | O | *e2i | 3A3 |
| 42 | 1.9 x 1.2 x 0.6 | – | O | e11 | 3A3 |
| 43 | 2.0 x 1.4 x 0.95 | D5 | O | d2 | 3A3 |
| 44 | 1.5 x 1.0 x 0.6 | – | O | *d3 | 3A3 |
| 45 | 2.0 x 1.35 x 0.75 | *A6i | O | e10 | 3A3/7A2ai |

Table 1: continued

| C.N. | DIMENSIONS (cm) | HEAD | BACK | SIDE | DESIGN |
|------|-----------------|------|------|------|--------|
| 46 | 1.7 x 1.4 x 0.45 | – | O | e11 | 3A2 |
| 47 | 1.75 x 1.25 x 0.85 | *D8i | O | e11 | 3A2 |
| 48 | 1.75 x 1.25 x 0.9 | *D8i | O | e2 | 3A2 |
| 49 | 1.3 x 0.85 x 0.6 | – | O | e11 | 12A |
| 50 | 1.25 x 0.8 x 0.65 | – | O | e11 | 12A |
| 51 | 1.2 x 0.85 x 0.6 | – | O | – | 12A |
| 52 | 1.9 x 1.3 x 0.9 | *A6i | I | *d3 | 12A |
| 53 | 1.9 x 1.3 x 1.0 | – | dec | – | 12A |
| 54 | 1.6 X 1.15 X 0.8 | – | O | – | 12A |
| 55 | 2.05 x 1.6 x 1.0 | B2 | O | – | 12A |

# TYPOLOGICAL FEATURES OF WARD AND TUFNELL FEATURED IN THE TEXT

## HEAD TYPES

A:     LUNATE

| | |
|---|---|
| A4 | plain with horn |
| A5 | eyes shown by double lines |
| A6 | depressed head shown with and without eyes and horn |
| *A6(i) | depressed head shown with and without eyes and horn; detached |

B:     OPEN

| | |
|---|---|
| B2 | single or double "hour–glass" outline, horn sometimes shown |
| *B2(i) | "hour–glass" outline, triangular head enclosed within |
| B4 | "hour–glass" outline, rounded eyes extending outwards and sometimes joined to a depressed base line |

C:     SQUARE

| | |
|---|---|
| C7 | double side lines, sometimes with horn, eyes unmarked |

D:     TRAPEZOIDAL

| | |
|---|---|
| D1 | plain trapezoidal, eyes extended outwards |
| D3 | plain trapezoidal, with or without horn inside open outline ending in square extensions for eyes |
| *D3(i) | as D3 with open base line |
| *D4(i) | plain trapezoidal with additional markings |
| D5 | double side lines, with or without horn |
| *D5(i) | as D5 with open base line |
| D6 | double side lines, with horn or squared eyes |
| D8 | triangle, with or without horn, sometimes with double lines, no eyes represented |
| *D8(i) | As D8 with eyes represented |

## BACK TYPES

| | |
|---|---|
| O | Plain |
| dec | Decorated |
| I | one line dividing the elytra |

## LEG TYPES

| | |
|---|---|
| d | chip carved, squared profile, legs meet where pronotum and elytra join |
| *d3 | rear leg indicated, plain |
| d13 | fore leg notched, mid leg fringed |
| | |
| e | scored, squared profile, base grooved, legs shown by grooving, notching or fringing |
| e2 | groove incomplete, hind leg diagonal |
| *e2i | as e2, with feathering |
| e5 | groove incomplete, hind leg marked |
| e9 | hind leg diagonal, for and/or hind leg notched |
| e10 | complete groove, straight notches on fore and hind legs |
| e11 | complete groove, no markings |
| *e11i | complete groove, feathering |

## BASE DESIGNS

| 1 | | Linear Pattern |
|---|---|---|
| *1B1 | | geometric |
| | | |
| 2 | | Scrolls and Spirals |
| | 2B2 | round, interlocking spirals, unending |
| | | |
| 3 | | Egyptian Signs and Symbols |
| 3A | | monograms and varia |
| | 3A2 | nb.ty with plants |
| | 3A3 | varia |
| 3B | | symmetic patterns |
| | 3B6 | GOLD–sign (nbw) in longitudinal setting |
| | 3B8 | flanking papyri |
| | *3B8(i) | single flanking |

61

## Base Designs cont'd.

**Base Designs cont'd.**

|  | 10C1a | human headed; holding palm |
|---|---|---|
| 10D |  | goddess |
| *10D3 |  | "naked–goddess" |

| 11 | Names and Titles |
|---|---|
| 11A | royal names |

| 12 | Unclassified or Uninscribed |
|---|---|

# ABBREVIATIONS

| | |
|---|---|
| AASOR | Annual of American School of Oriental Research |
| ADAIK | Abhandlungen des Deutschen Archäogischen Instituts Kairo |
| ADAJ | Annual of Department of Antiquities of Jordan |
| AJA | American Journal of Archaeology |
| | |
| BASOR | Bulletin of American School of Oriental Research |
| BAR | British Archaeological Reports |
| | |
| CdE | Chronique d'Egypt |
| CN | Catalogue Number |
| | |
| IEJ | Israel Exploration Journal |
| | |
| JEA | Journal of Egyptian Archaeology |
| JNES | Journal of Near Eastern Studies |
| JSSEA | Journal of the Society for the Study of Egyptian Antiquities |
| | |
| OBO | Orbis Biblicus et Orientalis |
| | |
| PEF | Palestine Exploration Fund |
| PEQ | Palestine Exploration Quarterly |
| | |
| ZÄS | Zeitschrift für ägyptische Sprache und Altertumskunde |
| ZDPV | Zeitschrift des Deutschen Palästina – Vereins |

# BIBLIOGRAPHY

ALBRIGHT, W.F., 1929 Progress in Palestinian Archaeology during the year 1928. *BASOR* 33, 1–10.
––– 1938 Tell Beit Mirsim II – The Bronze Age. *AASOR* 6, 13–74.

AMIRAN, R./EITAN, A., 1965 A Canaanite–Hyksos city at Tell Nagila. *Archaeology* 18, 113–123.

ANDREU, G., 1987 Les Scarabees in: Villa, A., *Le Cimetière Kermaïque D'Ukma Ouest*. Paris, 225–279.

AVI–YONAH, M./STERN, E., 1975 *Encyclopedia of Archaeological Excavations in the Holy Land I–IV*. London.

BECKERATH, J. von, 1964 *Untersuchungen zur politischen Geschichte der Zweiten Zwischenzeit in Ägypten*. Glückstadt.
––– 1984 *Handbuch der ägyptischen königsnamen*. MÄS. München/Berlin.

BEITZEL, B.J., 1985 *The Moody Atlas of Bible Lands*. Chicago.

BESTE, I., 1978 *Skarabäen*. Teil 1–3. CAA–Lose–Blatt Katalog Ägyptischer Altertumer. Kestner–Museum–Hannover, Mainz/Rhein.

BIETAK, M., 1979 Avaris and Piramesse. Archaeological Exploration in the Eastern Nile Delta. Mortimer Wheeler Archaeological Lecture 1979. From the *Proceedings of the British Academy*. London, vol lxv, 225–290.
––– 1984 Problems of the Chronology of the Middle Bronze Age: New Evidence from Egypt. *AJA* 88, 471–485.
––– 1989 The Middle Bronze Age of the Levant – A New Approach to Relative and Absolute Chronology. *High, Middle or Low? Acts of an International Colloqiuim on Absolute Chronology held at the University of Gothenburg, 20th–22nd August 1987. Part 3*. Åström, P.(ed.). Gothenburg.

---   1991   Egypt and Canaan during the Middle Bronze Age. *BASOR* 281, 27–72.

BIMSON, J.J., 1981 *Redating the Exodus and Conquest.* Sheffield.

BOURKE, S.J.B., 1989   Pella in the Bronze and Iron Ages. in: Hennessy et alii, Pella. *Archaeology of Jordan II.* Leuvan 1989, 414–424.

BRANDL, B., 1986   The Scarabs from Field VI at Gezer, in: Dever, W.G.(ed.), *Gezer IV: The 1969–1971 Seasons in Field VI, the 'Acropolis', Part 1: Text.* Jerusalem, 247–257.

BRIEND, J./ HUMBERT, J.B., 1980   *Tell Keisan (1971–1976). Une Cité phénicienne en Galilée.* OBO (Series Archaeologica 1). Freiburg/Göttingen/Paris.

BRUNTON, G., 1930   *Qau and Badari III.* London.

BRUNTON, G./ ENGELHART, G., 1927   *Gurob.* London.
---   1929–31 *Matmar. Vol I.* London.

BUCHANAN, B., 1966   *Catalogue of the Ancient Near Eastern Seals in the Ashmolean Museum. Vol 1: Cylinder Seals.* Oxford.

COLLON, D., 1981   The Aleppo Workshop. A Seal Cutter's Workshop in Syria in the Second Half of the 18th Century BC. *Ugarit Forschungen* 13, 33–43.
---   1982   *The Alalakh Cylinder Seals. A New Catalogue of the Actual Seals excavated by Sir Leonard Woolley at Tell Atchana, and from Neighbouring Sites on the Syrian–Turkish Border.* BAR International Series 132, Oxford.
---   1985   A North Syrian Cylinder Seal Style: Evidence of North–South Links with Ajjul. in: Tubb, J.N.(ed.) *Palestine in the Bronze and Iron Ages. Papers in Honour of Olga Tufnell.* London, 57–68.
---   1987   *First Impressions. Cylinder Seals in the Ancient Near East.* British Museum Publications.

O'CONNOR, D., 1985   The Chronology of Scarabs of the Middle Kingdom and the Second Intermediate Period. *JSSEA* 15/1, 1–41.

DE CLERCQ, L./MENANT, J., 1888   *Collection De Clercq – Catalogue méthodique raisonneé, Antiquités assyriennes I, Clyinderes orientaux*. Paris.

DEVER, W.G., 1985   Relations between Syria–Palestine and Egypt in the Hyksos Period. in: Tubb, J.N.(ed.), *Palestine in the Bronze and Iron Ages. Papers in Honour of Olga Tufnell*. London.
---   1990   "Hyksos" Egyptian Destructions, and the End of the Palestinian Middle Bronze Age. *LEVANT* XXII, 75–81.
---   1991   Tell el-Dab'a and Levantine Middle Bronze Age Chronology: A Rejoinder to Manfred Bietak. *BASOR* 281, 73–80.

DUMORTIER, J.-B., 1974   *Les Scarabées de Tell el Far'ah*. Unpublished disseration of the École Biblique et Archéologique, Jerusalem.

DUNAND, M., 1937   *Fouilles de Byblos I. 1926–32: Atlas*. Paris.

EMERY, W.B./KIRWAN L.P., 1935   *The Excavations and Survey between Wadi es–Sebua and Adindan 1929–31. 2 Vols*. Cairo.

ENGBERG, R.M., 1939   *The Hyksos Reconsidered*. Chicago.

ENGLEBACH, R./ GUNN, B., 1923   *Harageh*. London.

ERIKSSON, K., (Forthcoming)   Red Lustrous Wheel–made Ware: a product of Late Bronze Age Cyprus. in: *Cypriot Ceramics: Reading the Prehistoric Record*. The University Museum of Pennsylvania Philadelphia.

FRANKFURT, H., 1939   *Cylinder Seals. A Documentary Essay on the Art and Religion of the Ancient Near East*. London.

GIVEON, R., 1974   Hyksos Scarabs with Names of Kings and Officials from Canaan. *CdE* 98, 222–233.

---   1975   New Egyptian Seals with Titles and Names from Canaan. *TEL AVIV* 3, 127–133.

---   1977   Egyptian Finger Rings and Seals from South of Gaza. *TEL AVIV* 4, 66–70.

---   1978   *The Impact of Egypt on Canaan. Iconographical and Related Studies.* OBO 20, Freiburg/Schweiz and Göttingen.

--   1980a   A New Hyksos King. *TEL AVIV* 7, 90–91

---   1980b   Some Scarabs from Canaan with Egyptian Titles. *TEL AVIV* 7, 179–184.

---   1981   Some Egyptological Considerations concerning Ugarit. in: Young, G.D.(ed.), *Ugarit in Retrospect*, 55–58.

---   1983   The Hyksos in the South. in: *Fontes atque Pontes. Eine Festausgabe für Hellmut Brunner*, Wiesbaden, 155–161.

---   1985   *Egyptian Scarabs from Western Asia from the Collections of the British Museum.* OBO (Series Archaeologica 3), Freiburg/Schwiez and Göttingen.

---   1986   New Material Concerning Canaanite Gods in Egypt. *Proceedings of the IXth World Congress of Jewish Studies, Jerusalem: Division A.* Jerusalem, 1–4.

---   1988   *Scarabs from Recent Excavations in Israel.* OBO 83, Freiburg/Schweiz and Göttingen. (eds. Warburton, D./ Uehlinger, C.)

GIVEON, R./KERTESZ, T., 1986   *Egyptian Scarabs and Seals from Acco. From the Collections of the Israel Department of Antiquities and Museums.* Freiburg/Schweiz.

GRANT, E., 1932   *Ain Shems Excavations II.* Haverford.

GRIFFITH, F., 1890   The Antiquities of Tell el–Yahudiyeh. In: Naville, E., *The Mound of the Jew and the City of Onias.* London.

---   1923   *Oxford Excavations in Nubia.* Vol.4, Liverpool.

GUY, P.L.O., 1938   *Megiddo Tombs.* OIP 33, Chicago.

HABACHI, L., 1972 The Second Stele of Kamose and his Struggle against the Hyksos Ruler and his Capital. *ADAIK* 8, Glückstadt.

HALL, H.R., 1913 *Catalogue of Egyptian Scarabs in the British Museum. Vol I. Royal Scarabs*. London.

HAYES, W.C., 1968 *The Scepter of Egypt, Part II: The Hyksos Period and the New Kingdom*. New York.
--- 1973 Egypt from the death of Ammenemes III to Seqenenre III. *Cambridge Ancient History. Vol II.1*. Cambridge.

HENNESSY, J.B., 1985 Chocolate-on-white ware at Pella. in: Tubb, J.N.(ed.), *Palestine in the Bronze and Iron Ages. Papers in Honour of Olga Tufnell*. London.

HELCK, W., 1962 *Die Beziehungen Ägyptens au Vorderasien im 3. und. 2. Jahrtausend v. Chr*. Wiesbaden.
--- 1968 *Geschichte das alten Ägypten*. Leiden.

HERZOG, Z./ RAPP, G./ NEGBI, O.(eds), 1989 *Excavations at Tell Michal, Israel*. Minneapolis.

HESTRIN, R., 1987 The Lachish-Ewer and Asherah. *IEJ* 37, 212–214.
--- 1991 Understanding Asherah: Exploring Semetic Icongraphy. *Biblical Archaeology Review 17*, 50–59.

HOFFMEIER, J.K., 1989 Reconsidering Egypt's part in the Termination of the Middle Bronze Age in Palestine. *LEVANT* XXI, 181–193.
--- 1990 Some thoughts on William G. Dever's "Hyksos", Egyptian Destructions, and the End of the Palestinian Middle Bronze Age. *LEVANT* XXII, 83–9.
--- 1991 James Weinstein's 'Egypt and the Middle Bronze IIC/Late Bronze IA Transition in Palestine': A Rejoinder. *LEVANT* XXIII, 117–124.

HORN, S., 1962 Scarabs from Shechem. *JNES* 21, 1–14
--- 1966 Scarabs from Shechem. *JNES* 25, 48–56
--- 1973 Scarabs from Shechem. *JNES* 32, 281–289

HORNBLOWER, C.D., 1922 Some Hyksos Plaques and Scarabs. *JEA* 8, 201–208.

HORNUNG, E./ STAEHELIN, E., 1976 *Skarabäen und andere Siegelamulette aus Basler Sammlungen.* Mainz.

KAPLAN, J., 1955 A Cemetery of the Bronze Age discovered near Tel Aviv Harbour. *ATIQOT* 1, 1–18.

KEEL, O./ SCHROER. S., 1985 *Studien zu den Stempelsiegeln aus Palästina/Israel. Band I.* OBO 67, Freiburg/Schweiz and Göttingen.

KEEL, O./ KEEL-LEU, H./ SCHROER, S., 1989 *Studien zu den Stempelsiegeln aus Palästina/ Israel. Band II.* OBO 88, Freiburg/ Schweiz and Göttingen.

KEEL, O./ SHUVAL, M./ UEHLINGER, C., 1990 *Studien zu den Stempelsiegeln aus Palästina/Israel. Band III.* Freiburg/ Schweiz and Göttingen.

KEMPINSKI, A., 1974 Tell el-'Ajjul – Beth–Aglayim or Sharuhen?, *IEJ* 24, 145–152.
--- 1985 Some Observations on the Hyksos (XVth) Dynasty and its Canaanite Origins. in: Israelit–Groll, S.(ed.), *Pharaonic Egypt: The Bible and Christianity.* Jerusalem. 129–137.
--- 1988 *Excavations at Kabri. Preliminary Report of 1987 Season.* Tel Aviv.

KENYON, K., 1960 *Jericho I. The Tombs excavated 1952–1954.* London.
--- 1965 *Jericho II. The Tombs excavated 1955–1958.* London.

––– 1973 Palestine in the Middle Bronze Age. *Cambridge Ancient History, Vol II.I*, 77–116.

KIRKBRIDE, D., 1965 Scarabs; in: Kenyon, K., *Jericho II*. London.

LOUD, G., 1948 *Megiddo II – Seasons of 1935–1939*. 2 vols. OIP 62, Chicago.

LUCAS, A./ HARRIS, J.R., 1962 *Ancient Egyptian Materials and Industries*. London.

MACALISTER, R.A.S., 1912 *The Excavations of Gezer 1902–1905, 1907–1909*. 3 vols. London.

MACKAY, E.J.H./ MURRAY, M.A., 1952 *City of Sheperd Kings*. London.

MAGUIRE, L.C., 1991 *The Circulation of Cypriot Pottery in the Middle Bronze Age*. (unpublished PhD thesis, University of Edinburgh).

MARTIN, G.T., 1971 *Egyptian Administrative and Private Name Seals, Principally of Middle Kingdom and the Second Intermediate Period*. Oxford.

MATTHIAE, P., 1969 Empreintes d'un cylindre paléosyrien de Tell Mardikh. *SYRIA* 46, 1–43.

McNICOLL, A./SMITH, R./HENNESSY, J.B., 1982 *Pella in Jordan I*. Canberra.

McNICOLL, A., et alii, (in press) Pella in Jordan II. Sydney.

MLINAR, C., *Untersuchungen zu den Skarabäen der 2. Zwischenzeit.* (unpublished, Institute of Egyptology, Vienna)

MURRAY, M.A., 1949  Some Canaanite Scarabs. *PEQ* 81, 92–99.

NAVILLE, E., 1890  *Mound of the Jew and City of the Oasis*. London.

NEWBERRY, P.E., 1906  *Scarabs, an Introduction to the study of Egyptian Seals and Signet Rings*. London.
— — —  1907  *Scarab Shaped Seals*. London.

NICCACCI, A., 1980  *Hyksos Scarabs*. Studium Biblicum Franciscanum, Museum 2; Jerusalem.

PETRIE, W.M.F., 1886  *Naukratis I, Part I*. London.
— — —  1889  *Historical Scarabs*. London.
— — —  1890  *Kahun, Gurob, Hawara*. London.
— — —  1891  *Illahun, Kahun and Gurob*. London.
— — —  1906  *Hyksos and Isrealite Cities*. London.
— — —  1917  *Scarabs and Cylinders with Names*. London.
— — —  1919  *PEF Quarterly Statement*.
— — —  1925  *Button and Design Scarabs*. London.
— — —  1928  *Gerar*. London.
— — —  1930  *Beth Pelet I (Tell Fara)*. London.
— — —  1931  *Ancient Gaza I*. London.
— — —  1932  *Ancient Gaza II*. London.
— — —  1933  *Ancient Gaza III*. London.
— — —  1934  *Ancient Gaza IV*. London.
— — —  1952  *Ancient Gaza V*. London.

PETRIE, W.M.F./BRUNTON, G./MURRAY, M.A., 1923  *Lahun II*. London.

PORADA, E., 1948  *Corpus of Near Eastern seals in North American collections I, the Pierpont Morgan Library Collection*. Washington.

POTTS, T./COLLEDGE, S./EDWARDS, P., 1985 Preliminary Report on the 6th Season of Excavations by the University of Sydney at Pella in Joran (1983–1984). *ADAJ* XXIX, 181–210.

PRITCHARD, B., 1963 *The Bronze Age Cemetery at Gibeon.* Philadelphia.

REISNER, G.A., 1923 *Excavations at Kerma, Parts IV–V.* Harvard African Studies. Vol VI. Cambridge., Mass.
——— 1955 Clay Sealings of Dynasty XIII from Uronarti Fort. *KUSH* 3, 26–69

ROWE, A., 1936 *A Catalogue of Scarabs, Scaraboids, Seals and Amulets in the Palestine Archaeological Museum.* Cairo.

SAGONA, A.G., 1980 Middle Bronze Age Faience Vessels from Palestine. *ZDPV* 96, 101–120.

SCHAEFFER, C.F.A., 1939 *The Cuneiform Texts of Ras Shamra – Ugarit.* London.
——— 1983 *Corpus I des cylindres – sceaux de Ras Shamra – Ugarit et d'Enkomi – Alasia.* Paris

SCHROER, S., 1985 Der Mann im Wulstsaummentel. Ein Motiv der Mittlebronzezeit IIB. in: Keel, O./ Schroer, S., *Studien zu den Stempelsiegeln aus Palästina/Israel. Band I.* OBO 67, Freiburg/Schweiz and Göttingen., 49–107.
——— 1989 Die Göttin auf den Stempelsiegeln aus Palästina/ Israel. in: Keel, O./ Keel-Leu, H./ Schroer, S., *Studien zu den Stempelsiegeln aus Palästina/Israel. Band II.* OBO 88, Freiburg/Schweiz and Göttingen, 89–212.

SCHULMAN, A.R., 1975 The Ossimo scarab reconsidered. *Journal of the American Research Centre in Egypt* 12, 15–18.
——— 1978 Two Scarab Impressions from Tel Michal. *TEL AVIV* 5, 148–151.

SETERS, J. VAN, 1966  *The Hyksos: A New Investigation*. New Haven–London.

SMITH, H.S./ SMITH, A., 1976  A Reconsideration of the Kamose Texts. *ZÄS* 103, 48–76.

STARKEY, J.L./HARDING, L., 1932  *Beth Pelet II*. London.

STEINDORFF, G., 1937  *Aniba II*. Glückstadt.

STEWART, J.R., et al, 1974  *Tell el–'Ajjul: The Middle Bronze Age Remains*. (Studies in Mediterranean Archaeology 38, Göteborg).

STOCK, H., 1942  *Studien zur Geschichte und Archäologie der 13.– 17. Dyn. Ägyptens unter Berücksichigung der Skarabäen dieser Zwischenzeit*. New York.

TUFNELL, O., 1940  *Lachish II*. The Fosse Temple. London.
———    1953  *Lachish III*. London.
———    1956  'Hyksos' Scarabs from Canaan. *Anatolian Studies VI*, 67–74.
———    1958  *Lachish IV*. London.
———    1970  Some Scarabs with Decorated Backs. *LEVANT* 2, 95–99.
———    1973  The Middle Bronze Age Scarab–Seals from Burial on the Mound at Megiddo. *LEVANT* 5, 69–82.
———    1975a  Seal Impressions from Kahun and Uronarti Fort. *JEA* 61, 67–101.
———    1975b  Scarab Seals in Egypt and Palestine during the 2nd Intermediate Period. *Actes XXIXe Congrès des Orientalists, 104*.
———    1975/6  Tomb 66 at Ruweise, near Sidon, *BERYTUS* 24, 5–25.
———    1984  *Studies on Scarab Seals, Vol II. Scarab Seals and their Contribution to History in the Early Second Millennium BC*. Warminster.

VERCOUTTER, J., 1976 *Mirgissa III*. Paris.

WARD, W. 1978 *Studies on Scarab Seals, Vol I. Pre–12th Dynasty Scarab Amulets*. Warminster.

——— 1984 Royal–Name Scarabs. in: Tufnell, O; *Studies on Scarab Seals, Vol II. Scarab Seals and their Contribution to History in the Early Second Millennium BC*. Warminster.

——— 1987 Scarab Typology and Archaeological Context. *AJA* 91, 507–532.

WEILL, R., 1953 *XIIe dynastie, royaute de Haute–Egypt et domination hyksos dans le Nord*. Cairo.

WEINSTEIN, J.M., 1975 Egyptian Relations with Palestine in the Middle Kingdom. *BASOR* 217, 1–16.

——— 1981 The Egyptian Empire in Palestine: A Reassessment. *BASOR* 241.

——— 1991 Egypt and the Middle Bronze IIC/ Late Bronze IA Transition in Palestine. *LEVANT* XXIII, 105–115.

WILLIAMS, B., 1970 *Representational Scarabs from the 2nd Intermediate Period*. MA Thesis (unpublished), The University of Chicago.

——— 1975 *Archaeological and Historical Problems of the 2nd Intermediate Period*. Ph.D.Thesis (unpublished), University of Chicago.

WINTER, U., 1983 *Frau und Göttin. Exegetische und ikonographische. Studien zum weiblichen Gottesbild im Alten Israel und in dessen Umwelt*. OBO 53, Freiburg/ Schwiez and Göttingen.

# Catalogue of Scarabs from Tomb 62

# THE CATALOGUE

This catalogue has tried to present as much information as possible for further research. Thus it was of the highest priority to provide a detailed description, and three views in both drawings and photographs of each scarab.

Unfortunately, due to circumstances beyond my control, there is no drawing of the back and sides of CN 2, and no photographs of the back and sides of the following: CN 1, 2, 4 and 41. CN 31, 42 and 44 were drawn from photographs.

The catalogue is arranged in the following manner. A full description of each scarab is given, information divided amongst the following categories:

| | | |
|---|---|---|
| **C.N.** | : | Number in this catalogue (page no. in text, plate no.) |
| **LOCATION** | : | Site reference area. |
| **R.N.** | : | Registration number given on site to registered objects. |
| **DIMENSIONS** | : | Length x breadth x height. Given in cm. |
| **CONDITION** | : | State of preservation of scarab. |
| | | **Complete**: signifies in one piece. |
| | | **Intact**: signifies (probable) original condition, complete with glaze. |
| **SURFACE FINISH** | : | Condition of surface; extent and condition of glaze; if surface is polished or weathered. |
| **MATERIAL** | : | Substance of manufacture. |
| **DESCRIPTION** | : | Description of object plus note of piercing. |
| **BACK** | : | Description of head and back details. Wing cases are measured from front of head/clypeus. |
| **LEGS** | : | Description of side features. Note taken of feathering: RF: Right Front; LF: Left Front; RR: Right Rear; LR: Left Rear. (RHS: right hand side; LHS: left hand side). |
| **BASE** | : | Description of base design. |

All scarabs are drawn twice life size.

# THE CATALOGUE

| | |
|---|---|
| CN | 1 (p.9, pl.I) |
| LOCATION | T.62 1.2 |
| RN | 70367 |
| DIMENSIONS | 1.95 x 1.35 x 0.85 cm |
| CONDITION | Complete; chip from front threading hole and front of clypeus. Small chip from base. |
| S. FINISH | Back surface matt. 'Polished' strip down centre of back. Glaze remains on left plate, back depression, leg impression and base. Base polished. |
| MATERIAL | Steatite. |
| COLOUR | Yellowish. |
| DESCRIPTION | Oval shaped scarab seal pierced longitudinally for threading. |
| BACK | Clypeus and head outlined by single incisions leaving them raised. No eyes marked. Single incision divides head and thorax. High, plain back, with two 'depressions' at top of prothorax. Wing cases indicated by single incisions on outer edge of back approx. half way down. No internal details. |
| LEGS | Delineated by three incisions. First and uppermost runs from front threading hole to rear. Second and lowest runs from front threading hole, widens midway and then stops approx. two thirds way around side. Third runs from rear threading to meet the uppermost incision approx. midway along. No feathering attempted. |
| BASE | Oval incised border surrounds design set down length of scarab. Slightly off centre, footed cartouche reads: $^c3-ws(r)-r^c$. At top, a $k_3$ is flanked by wilting papyri; below, the cartouche is flanked by two $^cnh$'s and $nfr$'s. |

| | |
|---|---|
| CN | 2 (p.11, pl.I) |
| LOCATION | T.62 1.G |
| RN | 70604 |
| DIMENSIONS | 1.9 x 1.3 x 0.85 cm |
| CONDITION | Complete. |
| S. FINISH | Glaze remains on back and plates. Matt surface. |
| MATERIAL | Steatite. |
| COLOUR | Brown with blue/green glaze. Beige base. |
| DESCRIPTION | Oval shaped scarab seal pierced longitudinally for threading. |
| BACK | Clypeus and head outlined by single incisions. Single incision divides head and thorax. Back plain. Wing cases indicated by single incisions on outer edge of back approx. half way down. No internal details. |
| LEGS | Delineated by two single incisions running around thickness of scarab from front threading hole to rear. No feathering attempted. |
| BASE | Oval incised border surrounds hieroglyphs between a 'panel' border. Hieroglyphs read from top to bottom $ntr$ $nfr$ $nbw-wsr-r^c$ $dí$ $^cnh$. |

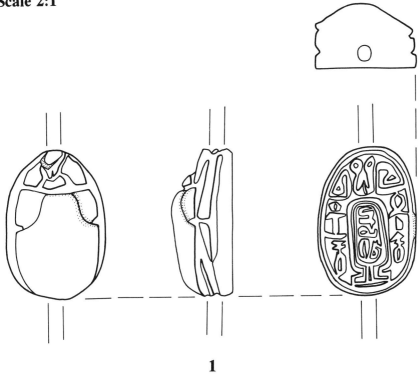

**1**

**2**

| | |
|---|---|
| CN | 3 (p.13, pl.I) |
| LOCATION | T.62 1.E |
| RN | 70410 |
| DIMENSIONS | 1.5 x 1.0 x 0.75 cm |
| CONDITION | Complete; one small chip from base. |
| S. FINISH | Matt surface. Small amount of glaze in incisions. |
| MATERIAL | Faience. |
| COLOUR | White. |
| DESCRIPTION | Oval shaped scarab seal pierced longitudinally for threading. |
| BACK | Clypeus and head outlined by single incisions. Horn marked, no eyes. Single incision divides head and thorax. Back plain and high. Wing cases indicated by single incisions on outer edge of back approx. half way down. No internal details. |
| LEGS | Delineated by four incisions. First and uppermost, runs from front threading hole to rear. Second runs from front threading hole approx. two thirds way around side. Third runs from rear threading hole approx. one third way around side, above second incisions and below first incision. A fourth incision runs diagonally above the third incision and directly beneath the uppermost incision. Feathering occurs in three sections: FR:6; LF:7; RR:7; LR:7. |
| BASE | Oval incised border surrounds hieroglyphs. Central column reads $w_3d-r^c-hpr$. Flanked by a single, identical column on each side, reading: $Hr-nb/r(?)-k_3-nb/r$ (?). Lowest one third contains double *ureaus* enclosing two *nfr* signs. |

| | |
|---|---|
| CN | 4 (p.15, pl.I) |
| LOCATION | T.62 1.2 |
| RN | 70300 |
| DIMENSIONS | 1.6 x 1.5 x 0.8 cm |
| CONDITION | Complete. |
| S. FINISH | Matt back surface, base polished surface. Glaze remains on clypeus, plates, back and wing cases. |
| MATERIAL | Steatite. |
| COLOUR | Beige with white glaze patches on back and yellow glaze on clypeus, back, plates and wing cases. |
| DESCRIPTION | Oval shaped scarab seal pierced longitudinally for threading. |
| BACK | Clypeus outlined by incision leaving it raised. Eyes marked, no head indicated. Single incision divides head and thorax. Back plain. Wing cases indicated by single incisions on outer edge of back approx. half way down. No internal details. |
| LEGS | Delineated by two single incisions running around thickness of scarab from front threading hole to rear. No feathering attempted. |
| BASE | Oval incised border surrounds standing female figure, with long hair, with face to left. 'Branches' around inside of border. |

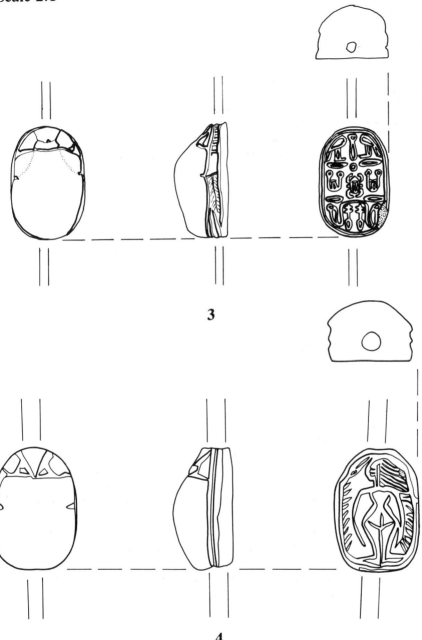

**3**

**4**

| | |
|---|---|
| CN | 5 (p.15, pl.I) |
| LOCATION | T.62 1.2 |
| RN | 70384 |
| DIMENSIONS | 1.75 x 1.15 x 0.7 cm (Base; 1.65 x 1.15) |
| CONDITION | Complete. |
| S. FINISH | No glaze remains. Matt surface. |
| MATERIAL | Steatite. |
| COLOUR | Beige; yellowy beige on back; off white–beige on base. |
| DESCRIPTION | Oval shaped scarab seal pierced longitudinally for threading. |
| BACK | Clypeus, head, eyes and plates outlined by single incisions leaving them raised. Horn marked. Wide, single incision divides head and thorax. Back plain. Wing cases indicated by single incisions on outer edge of back approx. half way down. No internal details. |
| LEGS | Delineated by two single incisions running around thickness of scarab from front threading hole to rear. No feathering attempted. |
| BASE | Design enclosed within incised oval border. Design comprises a standing female figure, head turned to the right. She is three quarters enclosed by a rope border. |

| | |
|---|---|
| CN | 6 (p.16, pl.II) |
| LOCATION | T.62 1.G |
| RN | 70493 |
| DIMENSIONS | 2.1 x 1.4 x 0.95 cm |
| CONDITION | Complete. |
| S. FINISH | No glaze remains. |
| MATERIAL | Steatite. |
| COLOUR | Pale brown. |
| DESCRIPTION | Oval shaped scarab seal pierced longitudinally for threading. |
| BACK | Clypeus, head and possibly eyes outlined by single incisions. Single incision divides head and thorax. Back plain. Wing cases indicated by single incisions on outer edge of back approx. half way down. No internal details. |
| LEGS | Delineated by two single incisions running around thickness of scarab from front threading hole to rear. No feathering attempted. |
| BASE | Oval incised border surrounds design running down length of scarab. Design comprises two figures, facing each other, standing on a *nb* sign. Figures have their arms behind them and knees bent. |

**Scale 2:1**

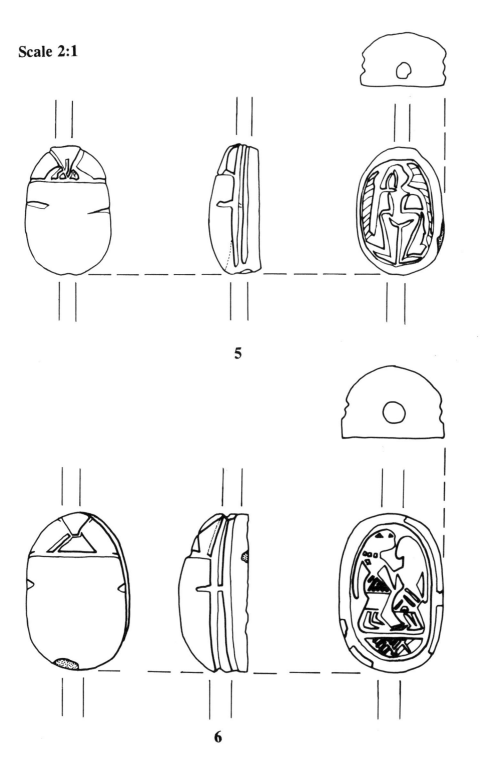

**5**

**6**

| | |
|---|---|
| CN | 7 (p.18, pl.II) |
| LOCATION | T.62 1.3 |
| RN | 70698 |
| DIMENSIONS | 2.0 x 1.35 x 0.85 cm |
| CONDITION | Complete; no glaze remains. |
| S. FINISH | Polished surface remains. |
| MATERIAL | Steatite. |
| COLOUR | Whitish; yellow/brown on back. |
| DESCRIPTION | Oval shaped scarab seal pierced longitudinally for threading. |
| BACK | Clypeus and eyes outlined by single incisions leaving them raised. No head represented. Single incision divides head area and thorax. Back plain. Wing cases indicated by single incisions on outer edge of back approx. two fifths way down. No internal details. |
| LEGS | Delineated by two single incisions running around thickness of scarab from front threading hole to rear. No feathering attempted. |
| BASE | Oval incised border surrounds design running down length of scarab. Design comprises a female figure, facing left, standing, holding a (palm) branch. Her body is hatched. |

| | |
|---|---|
| CN | 8 (p.19, pl.II) |
| LOCATION | T.62 3.G |
| RN | 70562 |
| DIMENSIONS | 1.5 x 1.05 x 0.65 cm |
| CONDITION | Complete; chips from rear threading hole, one extending to base. Chipped above front threading hole, leaving clypeus damaged. Several small chips around edge of base. Series of small cracks across back. |
| S. FINISH | Matt finish. Small amount of glaze visible on plates. |
| MATERIAL | Steatite. |
| COLOUR | Creamy white with brown patches and a grey core. Small amount of yellow glaze. |
| DESCRIPTION | Oval shaped scarab seal pierced longitudinally for threading. |
| BACK | Clypeus and head outlined by single incisions leaving them raised. Raised eyes barely visible. Plates defined by incisions around clypeus and those defining head and thorax. Back plain. Wing cases indicated by single incisions on outer edge of back approx. one third way down. No internal details. |
| LEGS | Delineated by two single incisions running around thickness of scarab from front threading hole to rear. No feathering attempted. |
| BASE | Oval border surrounds kneeling female figure facing right. Figure holds in her left hand a palm leaf, with top resembling a $w3s$ sceptre. Figure wears a long kilt decorated with hatching in two directions. |

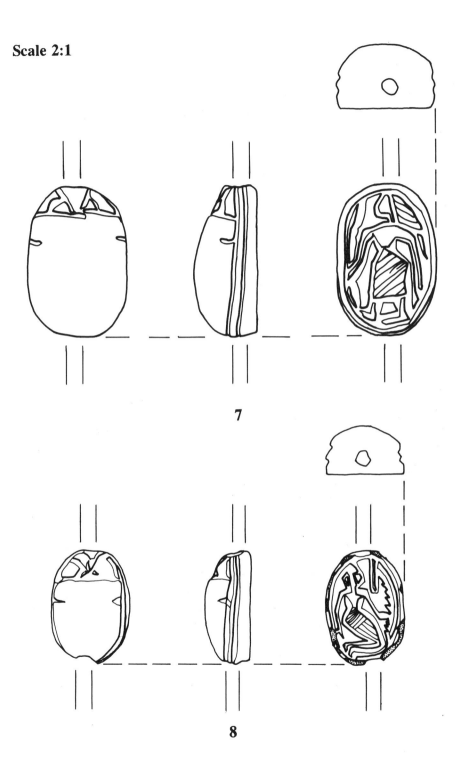

7

8

| | |
|---|---|
| CN | 9 (p.19, pl.II) |
| LOCATION | T.62 3.F |
| RN | 70928 |
| DIMENSIONS | 1.6 x 1.1 x 0.55 cm |
| CONDITION | Complete; shallow chip from middle of back and from base. |
| S. FINISH | Matt surface. |
| MATERIAL | Steatite. |
| COLOUR | Off-white with yellow/beige tinges on plates,back,sides and base. Brown patch on middle of back. |
| DESCRIPTION | Oval shaped scarab seal pierced longitudinally for threading. |
| BACK | Clypeus outlined by single incision leaving it raised. Head and eyes defined by shallow incisions. Single incision divides head and thorax. Back plain. Wing cases indicated by single incisions on outer edge of back approx. half (LHS) and one third (RHS) way down. No internal details. |
| LEGS | Delineated by two single incisions running around thickness of scarab, but only bottom incision joins both front threading hole and rear. No feathering attempted. |
| BASE | Incised oval border surrounds an incised female figure who kneels facing right. She holds a (stylised) palm leaf. |

| | |
|---|---|
| CN | 10 (p.19, pl.III) |
| LOCATION | T.62 1.G |
| RN | 70544 |
| DIMENSIONS | 2.0 x 1.45 x 0.95 cm |
| CONDITION | Complete; chips from head, side and base. |
| S. FINISH | Polished surface. |
| MATERIAL | Steatite. |
| COLOUR | Yellow. |
| DESCRIPTION | Oval shaped scarab seal pierced longitudinally for threading. |
| BACK | Clypeus, head and eyes outlined by single incisions. Single incision divides head and thorax. Back plain. Wing cases indicated by single incisions on outer edge of back approx. half way down. No internal details. |
| LEGS | Delineated by three incisions. First and uppermost runs from front threading hole to rear. Second and lowest runs from front threading hole, widens midway and finishes before rear threading hole. Third runs diagonally upwards from rear threading hole, to meet uppermost incision approx. one fifth way around side. No feathering attempted. |
| BASE | Oval incised border surrounds design running down length of scarab. Design comprises a skirted figure facing right, arms outstretched, gesturing. On RHS in front of figure is *ḫpr* beetle and *r* or *nb* sign. Behind figure is a *ureaus* and *r* or *nb* sign. |

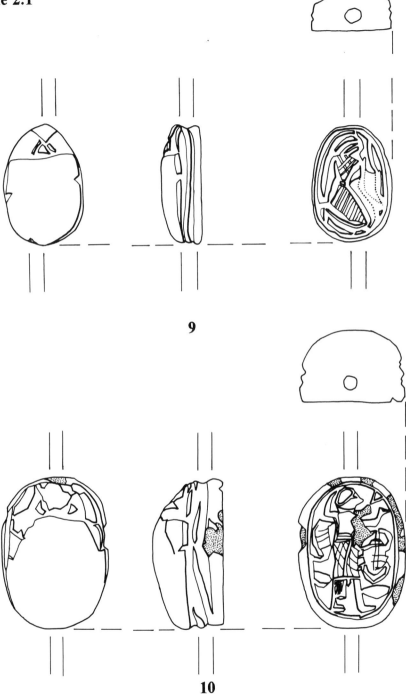

**9**

**10**

| CN | 11 (p.20, pl.III) |
|---|---|
| LOCATION | T.62 1.G |
| RN | 70666 |
| DIMENSIONS | 2.6 x 1.9 x 1.0 cm |
| CONDITION | Complete; chips on back, side and from border on base. |
| S. FINISH | Polished surface. |
| MATERIAL | Steatite. |
| COLOUR | Pale bluish/grey surface with darker interior. |
| DESCRIPTION | Oval shaped scarab seal pierced longitudinally for threading. |
| BACK | Clypeus, head and eyes outlined by single incisions leaving them raised. Single, wide incision divides head and thorax. Back is decorated with two incised lines that start at rear and run diagonally inwards, with notches/ feathering running off on inside. Wing cases indicated by single incisions on outer edge of back approx. half way down. No internal details. |
| LEGS | Delineated by three incisions. First and uppermost runs from front threading hole to rear. Second and lowest runs from front threading hole to rear. Third runs from rear threading hole, diagonally upwards and meets uppermost incision approx. half way around side. No feathering attempted. |
| BASE | Incised oval border surrounds design running down length of scarab. Design comprises two human figures. One, the larger, sits on a chair and is holding hands with the standing, smaller, figure. Both have hatched skirts and hair. |

| CN | 12 (p.22, pl.III) |
|---|---|
| LOCATION | T.62 1.J |
| RN | 70699 |
| DIMENSIONS | 1.7 x 1.2 x 0.8 cm |
| CONDITION | Complete; no remains of glaze. |
| S. FINISH | Matt finish. |
| MATERIAL | Steatite |
| COLOUR | Yellow. |
| DESCRIPTION | Oval shaped scarab seal pierced longitudinally for threading. |
| BACK | Clypeus and eyes outlined by single incisions leaving them raised. No head represented. Single incision divides head area and thorax. Back plain. Wing cases indicated by single incisions on outer edge of back approx. half way down. No internal details. |
| LEGS | Delineated by two single incisions running around thickness of scarab from front threading hole to rear. No feathering attempted. |
| BASE | Oval incised border surrounds design running across length of scarab. Incised design comprises goat facing right with a tree in front of front legs. Body of goat is incised. |

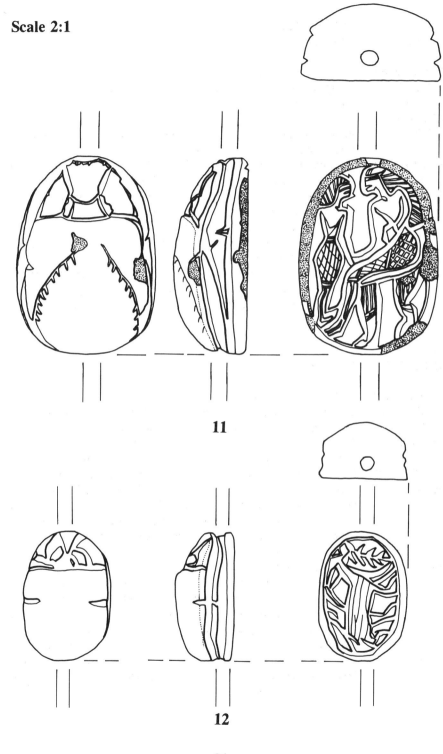

Scale 2:1

**11**

**12**

91

| | |
|---|---|
| CN | 13 (p.22, pl.III) |
| LOCATION | T.62 3.F |
| RN | 70925 |
| DIMENSIONS | 1.5 x 1.05 x 0.7 cm |
| CONDITION | Complete; chip from front threading hole, clypeus and base border. |
| S. FINISH | Matt surface. |
| MATERIAL | Steatite. |
| COLOUR | Beige with grey patch on back, side and base. Shiny dark beige patches visible on back and head. |
| DESCRIPTION | Oval shaped scarab seal pierced longitudinally for threading. |
| BACK | Clypeus, horn and eyes outlined by single incisions leaving them raised. Head lost but four incisions radiate from back of head towards prothorax. Two incisions divide head and back, running from side to middle, joining with head itself. Back plain. Wing cases indicated by single incisions on outer edge of back approx. one fifth (LHS) and one third (RHS) way down. No internal details. |
| LEGS | Delineated by two single incisions running around thickness of scarab from front threading hole to rear. No feathering attempted. |
| BASE | Oval incised border surrounds goat facing right. A ᶜ sign lies in top left corner. |

| | |
|---|---|
| CN | 14 (p.23, pl.IV) |
| LOCATION | T.62 3.G |
| RN | 70765 |
| DIMENSIONS | 1.85 x 0.8 x 0.75 cm |
| CONDITION | Complete; few chips from sides, base and front threading hole. |
| S. FINISH | Glaze remains over most of back, sides and base. |
| MATERIAL | Steatite. |
| COLOUR | Glaze light greeny/blue with darker blue patches. Brown underneath. |
| DESCRIPTION | Oval shaped scarab seal pierced longitudinally for threading. |
| BACK | Clypeus, head and plates outlined by single, deep incisions leaving them raised. No eyes marked. Single deep incision divides head and prothorax. Wing cases indicated by single incisions on outer edge of back approx. half way down. No internal details. Prothorax and elytra division marked. Elytra divided into two by a vertical incision. |
| LEGS | Delineated by three incisions. First runs from front threading hole to rear. Second and lowest runs from front threading hole, widens midway to a large triangular shape (which opens at the top to join uppermost incision) and stops approx. two thirds way around side. Third runs diagonally upwards, from rear threading hole to meet the uppermost incision approx. midway along. No feathering attempted. |
| BASE | Oval incised border surrounds design running down length of scarab. Design comprises goat (kneeling/lying) facing right with filling ornament above back in top left corner. |

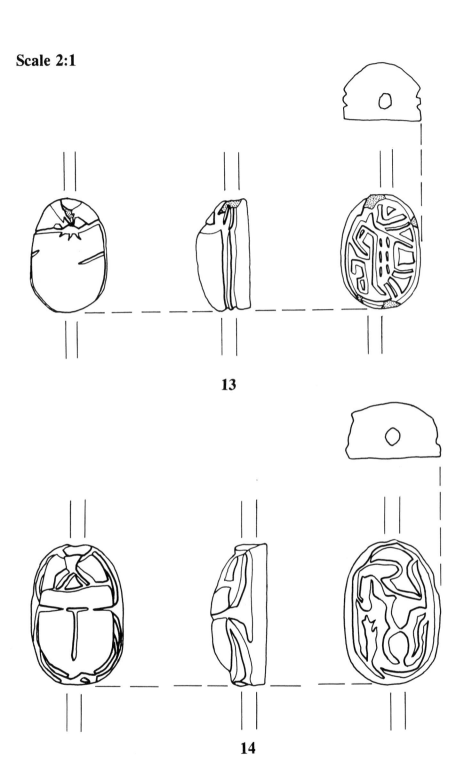

**Scale 2:1**

13

14

| | |
|---|---|
| CN | 15 (p.24, pl.IV) |
| LOCATION | T.62 3.1 |
| RN | 70563 |
| DIMENSIONS | 2.05 x 1.4 x 0.85 cm |
| CONDITION | Complete; small chips from back, sides and base. |
| S. FINISH | Matt surface. |
| MATERIAL | Steatite. |
| COLOUR | Yellow. |
| DESCRIPTION | Oval shaped scarab seal pierced longitudinally for threading. |
| BACK | Clypeus, head and possible eyes outlined by single incisions leaving them raised. Single incision divides head and thorax. Back plain. Wing cases indicated by single incisions on outer edge of back approx. one third way down. No internal details. |
| LEGS | Delineated by three incisions. First and uppermost runs from front threading hole to rear. Second and lowest runs from front threading hole, widens slightly midway, and stops approx. one third way around side. Third runs diagonally upwards from rear threading hole, to meet uppermost incision approx. midway along. No feathering attempted. |
| BASE | Incised, oval border surrounds design running across length of scarab. Incised design comprises a lion facing left flanked by two cobra's one above its back, the other in front of him. Internal hatching on bodies of all three figures. |

| | |
|---|---|
| CN | 16 (p.24, pl.IV) |
| LOCATION | T.62 3.I |
| RN | 70877 |
| DIMENSIONS | 2.0 x 1.45 x 0.9 cm (Base: 2.0 x 1.4) |
| CONDITION | Complete; numerous chips around base. |
| S. FINISH | Head and sides very chalky. |
| MATERIAL | Steatite. |
| COLOUR | Tones of beige/brown. Sides and part of head are chalky white. |
| DESCRIPTION | Oval shaped scarab seal pierced longitudinally for threading. |
| BACK | Clypeus outlined by single incision. Eyes and head are indistinguishable due to chalky substance. Single division divides head and thorax. Back plain. Wing cases indicated by single incisions on outer edge of back approx. half way down. No internal details. |
| LEGS | Delineated by two single, shallow incisions running around thickness of scarab from front threading hole to rear. No feathering attempted. |
| BASE | Design was surrounded by oval incised border but this has been chipped away. Design comprises a lion between two cobra's. Bodies of animals are hatched. Lion faces right, cobra faces inwards to lion. |

Scale 2:1

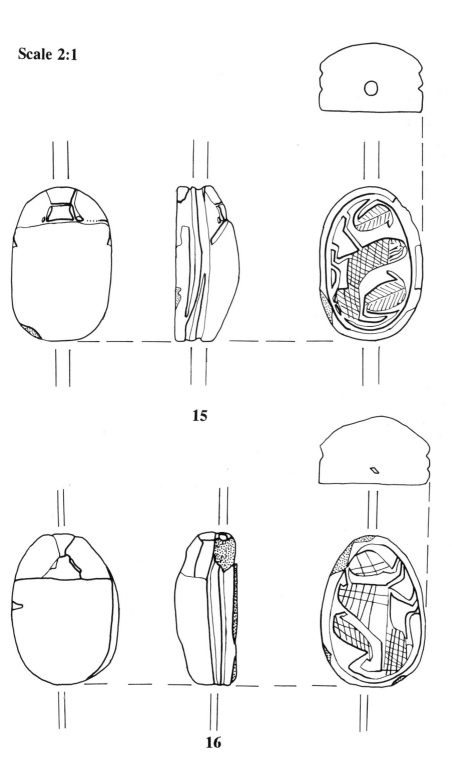

15

16

95

| | |
|---|---|
| CN | 17 (p.25, pl.IV) |
| LOCATION | T.62 3.H/I |
| RN | 70878 |
| DIMENSIONS | 1.6 x 1.15 x 0.65 cm |
| CONDITION | Complete. |
| S. FINISH | Matt surface. Faint remains of glaze. |
| MATERIAL | Steatite. |
| COLOUR | Yellow/brown with blue glaze. |
| DESCRIPTION | Oval shaped scarab seal pierced longitudinally for threading. |
| BACK | Clypeus, head, eyes and plates outlined by single incisions. Single incision divides head and thorax. Back plain. Wing cases indicated by single incisions on outer edge of back approx. half way down. No internal details. |
| LEGS | Delineated by two incisions. First runs from front threading hole to rear. Second begins at rear threading hole but finishes before wing case. No feathering attempted. |
| BASE | Oval incised border surrounds design which runs across length of scarab. Design comprises a $hpr$ beetle flanked by cobra's with an $r$ or $nb$ above. |

| | |
|---|---|
| CN | 18 (p.21/25, pl.V) |
| LOCATION | T.62 1.E |
| RN | 70399 |
| DIMENSIONS | 2.3 x 1.5 x 0.85 cm |
| CONDITION | Complete. |
| S. FINISH | Polished, some glaze remains. |
| MATERIAL | Steatite. |
| COLOUR | Beige; trace of white and blue glaze within figure, and both sets of cobra's and $nb$ signs. |
| DESCRIPTION | Rectangular shaped scaraboid/plaque pierced longitudinally for threading. |
| BACK | Incised oval border surrounds a female figure in low relief facing right with two cobra's in front, all above a $nb$ sign. |
| LEGS | Delineated by two single incisions running around thickness of scarab from front threading hole to rear. No feathering attempted. |
| BASE | $Hpr$ beetle flanked by two cobra's over a $nb$ sign. |

Scale 2:1

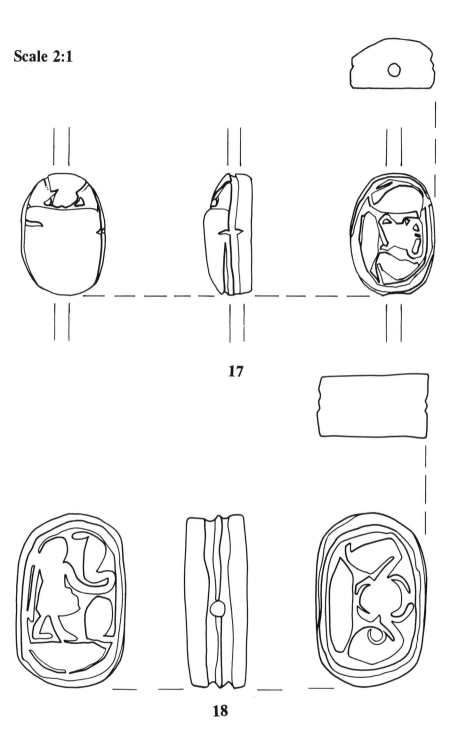

**17**

**18**

| | |
|---|---|
| CN | 19 (p.26, pl.V) |
| LOCATION | T.62 1.2 |
| RN | 70386 |
| DIMENSIONS | 1.65 x 1.15 x 0.8 cm |
| CONDITION | Complete; chip on back, base and left legs. |
| S. FINISH | Slightly polished, glaze remains on base. |
| MATERIAL | Steatite. |
| COLOUR | Beige, glaze white. |
| DESCRIPTION | Oval shaped scarab seal pierced longitudinally for threading. |
| BACK | Clypeus and head outlined by single incisions leaving them raised. Clypeus has five notches at front, and horn marked. Single incision divides head and thorax. Back plain and rounded. Wing cases indicated by single incisions on outer edge of back approx. half way down. No internal details. |
| LEGS | Delineated by three incisions. First and uppermost runs from front threading hole to rear. Second and lowest runs from front threading hole widens midway and then stops approx. two thirds way around side. Third runs diagonally upwards from rear threading hole, above lowest incision, to meet the uppermost incision approx. midway along. No feathering attempted. |
| BASE | Oval incised border surrounds a *ḫpr* beetle, in turn surrounded by a linked scroll design. |

| | |
|---|---|
| CN | 20 (p.26, pl.V) |
| LOCATION | T.62 4.D |
| RN | 70926 |
| DIMENSIONS | 1.9 x 1.35 x 0.85 cm |
| CONDITION | Complete; small chip from border of base. |
| S. FINISH | Matt surface. |
| MATERIAL | Steatite. |
| COLOUR | Yellow |
| DESCRIPTION | Oval shaped scarab seal pierced longitudinally for threading. |
| BACK | Clypeus, head and eye (?) outlined by single incisions leaving them raised. Single incision divides head and thorax. Back plain. Wing cases indicated by single incisions on outer edge of back approx. half way down. No internal details. |
| LEGS | Delineated by two single incisions running around thickness of scarab from front threading hole to rear. No feathering attempted. |
| BASE | Oval incised border surrounds design running across length of scarab. Design comprises a winged animal facing right with a cobra in front. |

Scale 2:1

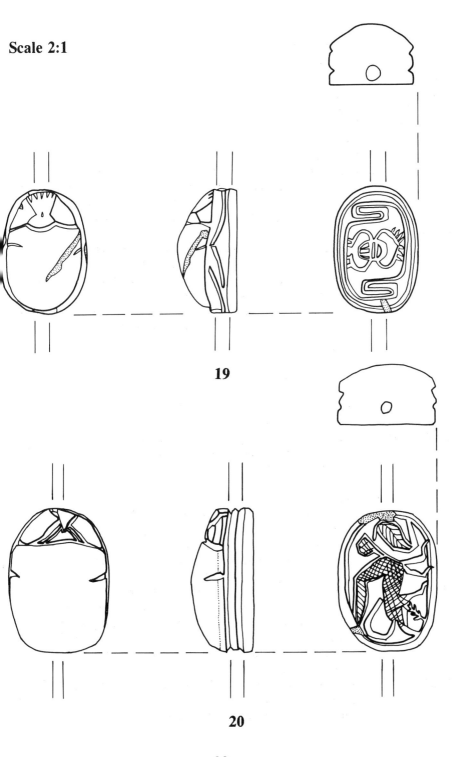

**19**

**20**

| | |
|---|---|
| CN | 21 (p.26, pl.V) |
| LOCATION | T.62 1.G |
| RN | 70608 |
| DIMENSIONS | 1.7 x 1.2 x 0.8 cm |
| CONDITION | Complete. |
| S. FINISH | Matt finish. |
| MATERIAL | Steatite. |
| COLOUR | Off white. |
| DESCRIPTION | Oval shaped scarab seal pierced longitudinally for threading. |
| BACK | Clypeus and head outlined by single incisions. Single incision divides head and thorax. Back plain. Wing cases indicated by single incisions on outer edge of back approx. half way down. No internal details. |
| LEGS | Delineated by three incisions. First and uppermost runs from front threading hole to rear. Second and lowest runs from front threading hole approx. two thirds way around side. Third runs from rear threading hole, diagonally upwards to meet uppermost incision approx. one third way around side. No feathering attempted. |
| BASE | Oval incised border surrounds design running down length of scarab. Design comprises a horus (?) sitting on a *nb* sign flanked by cobras with two cobras above. |

| | |
|---|---|
| CN | 22 (p.27, pl.V) |
| LOCATION | T.62 1.2 |
| RN | 70385 |
| DIMENSIONS | 1.75 x 1.2 x 0.75 cm |
| CONDITION | Complete; cracks across back and right side. Few chips from base. |
| S. FINISH | Extremely faint remains of glaze surrounding plates, and on sides. Matt surface remains. |
| MATERIAL | Steatite. |
| COLOUR | Light beige with brown patches. |
| DESCRIPTION | Oval shaped scarab seal pierced longitudinally for threading. |
| BACK | Clypeus, head and eyes outlined by single incisions leaving them raised. Horn marked. Single incision divides head and thorax. Back plain. Wing cases indicated by single incisions on outer edge of back approx. half way down. No internal details. |
| LEGS | Delineated by three incisions. First runs from front threading hole, diagonally upwards to approx. one third way around side. Second runs diagonally down from end of first incision, reaching almost to rear threading hole. Third runs from rear threading hole diagonally upwards, above second incision, to approx. one third way around side. No feathering attempted. |
| BASE | Oval incised border surrounds arrangement of hieroglyphs. Central column consists of three vertical *nfr* signs flanked by $^c-n-r$ motif. Signs in corner are possibly stylised lotus'. |

100

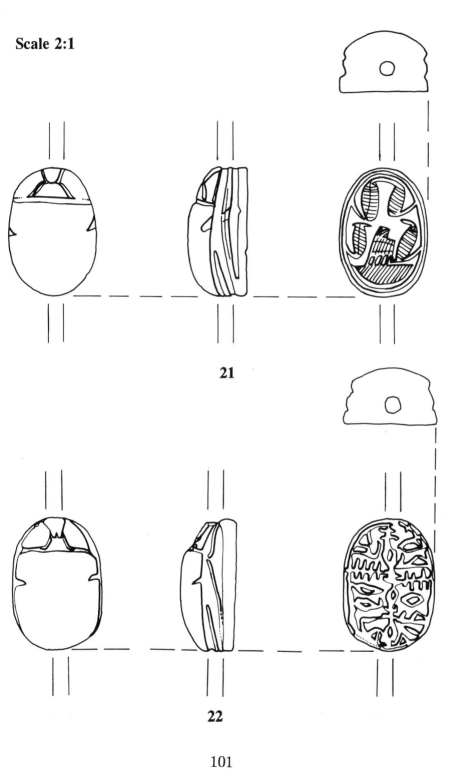

**21**

**22**

| | |
|---|---|
| CN | 23 (p.28, pl. VI) |
| LOCATION | T.62 1.F |
| RN | 70487 |
| DIMENSIONS | 1.3 x 2.0 x 0.9 cm |
| CONDITION | Complete; few chips from edge of base. |
| S. FINISH | Surface worn. Traces of blue/green glaze visible. |
| MATERIAL | Steatite. |
| COLOUR | Ivory. Dark brown patches at rear of back. |
| DESCRIPTION | Oval shaped scarab seal pierced longitudinally (slightly off centre), for threading. |
| BACK | Clypeus, head, eyes outlined by single incisions, which also divides head and thorax. Back decorated with lotus design with five petals. Wing cases indicated by single incisions on outer edge of back approx. half way down. No internal details. |
| LEGS | Delineated by three deep incisions. First and uppermost runs from front threading hole to rear. Second runs three quarters of side from front threading hole. Third runs to rear threading hole. Stylised feathering represented: RF:7; LF:7; RR:7; LR:7. |
| BASE | Oval border surrounds hieroglyphs in three panels, across width of scarab. From top: papyrus plant of lower Egypt flanked by two $ḥ^c$ signs. Then horizontally placed oval cartouche (incomplete) with $^c-n-r$ on top of double *ureaus* flanking $ḥ_ʒst$ above $ḥ^c$. |

| | |
|---|---|
| CN | 24 (p.28, pl. VI) |
| LOCATION | T.62 1.G |
| RN | 70564 |
| DIMENSIONS | 1.7 x 1.2 x 0.9 cm |
| CONDITION | Complete; badly chipped around threading holes, resulting in loss of clypeus at front. Back covered with fine cracks. |
| S. FINISH | Small amounts of glaze remain. |
| MATERIAL | Steatite. |
| COLOUR | Off white/light yellow. Grey/black on top of back and base. Tiny patches of turquoise/green glaze on clypeus and wing cases. |
| DESCRIPTION | Oval shaped scarab seal pierced longitudinally for threading. |
| BACK | Clypeus, head, eyes and plates outlined by single incisions leaving them raised. Single incision divides head and thorax. Back plain and very high. Wing cases indicated by single incisions on outer edge of back approx. half way down. No internal details. |
| LEGS | Delineated by two incisions. First and uppermost starts from just beyond the front threading hole and runs to the rear. Second runs from front threading hole to rear, widening slightly midway to form a triangular shape. Rear leg has four small diagonal incisions. |
| BASE | Incised oval border surrounds hieroglyphs. Design leads across field of base:$^c-n-r$ design surrounds central motif comprising a *nsw-bity* (reading R-L), with an $^cnḥ$ (?) sign under the combined *nsw* and head of bee, and a *nfr* sign (under *bity*). Below a large *nwb* sign. |

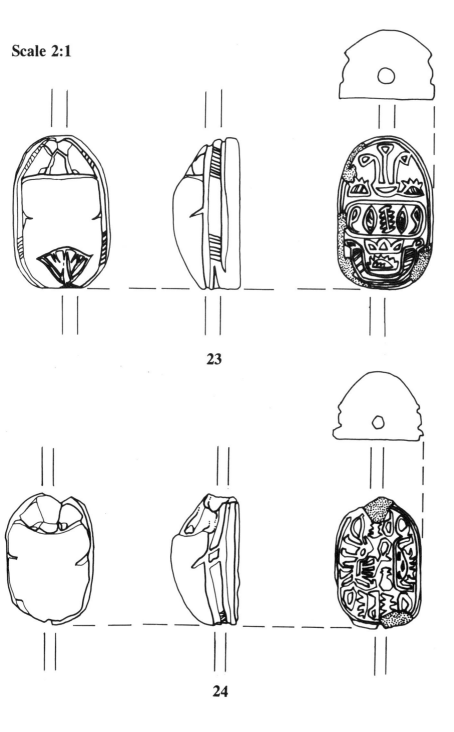

**Scale 2:1**

23

24

| | |
|---|---|
| CN | 25 (p.29, pl.VI) |
| LOCATION | T.62 3.G |
| RN | 70791 |
| DIMENSIONS | 1.9 x 1.3 x 0.85 cm (Base: 1.8 x 1.3) |
| CONDITION | Complete; LHS badly chipped. |
| S. FINISH | Weathered and cracked. Traces of glaze around clypeus. |
| MATERIAL | Steatite. |
| COLOUR | Off white/cream surface patches of light brown (esp. on back). Beige in break. Glaze is an off–white. |
| DESCRIPTION | Oval shaped scarab seal pierced longitudinally for threading. |
| BACK | Clypeus raised. Head outlined with thin, raised ridge. Eyes raised and form termination points for ridge. High, plain back. Wing cases indicated by single incisions on outer edge of back approx. half way down. No internal details. |
| LEGS | Delineated by two single incisions running around thickness of scarab from front threading hole to rear. No feathering attempted. |
| BASE | Oval incised border surrounds hieroglyphic design running down length of scarab. From top: $r-\varsigma-n-sn-\varsigma-r$ in centre field. Surrounded by vertical lines with central horizontal nicks. LHS:5; RHS:7. |

| | |
|---|---|
| CN | 26 (p.29, pl.VI) |
| LOCATION | T.62 1.G |
| RN | 70611 |
| DIMENSIONS | 2.6 x 1.8 x 1.15 cm |
| CONDITION | Complete; chips from base. |
| S. FINISH | Polished surface. |
| MATERIAL | Steatite. |
| COLOUR | Yellow/white. |
| DESCRIPTION | Oval shaped scarab seal pierced longitudinally for threading. |
| BACK | Clypeus, head and eyes outlined by single incisions leaving them raised. Single incision divides head and thorax. Back plain. Wing cases indicated by single incisions on outer edge of back approx. half way down. No internal details. |
| LEGS | Delineated by three incisions. First and uppermost runs from front threading hole to rear. Second and lowest runs from front threading hole widening to a triangular shape approx. one third way along side. Third runs from rear threading hole, diagonally upwards to meet uppermost incision joining it approx. midway along side. No feathering attempted. |
| BASE | Incised oval, hatched border surrounds design which runs down length of scarab. Design comprises (from top to bottom): $\varsigma nh$ flanked by $Hr$ falcons standing on $nb$ signs, above a rectangular 'shrine' enclosing the letters $htp-n-r-n-r$. Shrine flanked by $\varsigma nh$ signs with possible squared off corners or sideway crowns of Upper Egypt. |

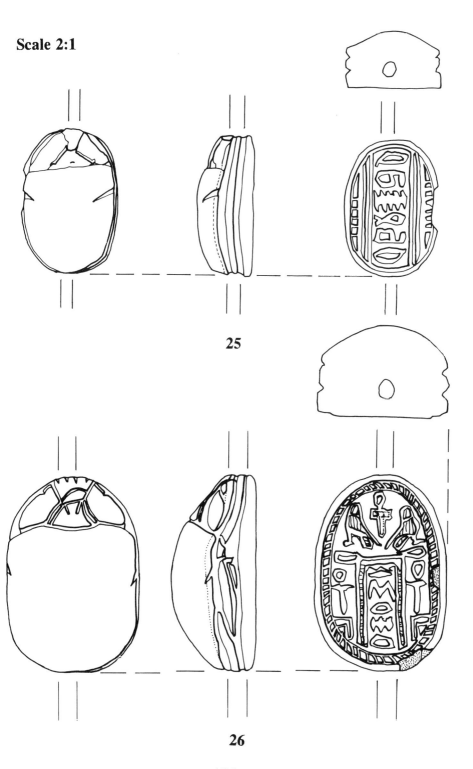

**Scale 2:1**

**25**

**26**

| | |
|---|---|
| CN | 27 (p.32, pl.VII) |
| LOCATION | T.62 1.E |
| RN | 70530 |
| DIMENSIONS | 1.9 x 1.4 x 0.85 cm |
| CONDITION | Complete. |
| S. FINISH | Matt surface. No glaze remains. |
| MATERIAL | Steatite. |
| COLOUR | Yellow. |
| DESCRIPTION | Oval shaped scarab seal pierced longitudinally for threading. |
| BACK | Clypeus and head outlined by single incisions leaving them raised. Single incision divides head and thorax. Back plain. Wing cases indicated by single incisions on outer edge of back approx. half way down. No internal details. |
| LEGS | Delineated by three incisions. First and uppermost runs from front threading hole to rear. Second and lowest runs from front threading hole approx. two thirds way around side. Third runs diagonally upwards from rear threading hole to meet uppermost incision approx. midway. No feathering attempted. |
| BASE | Oval incised border surrounds 'butterfly' design, running down length of scarab. |

| | |
|---|---|
| CN | 28 (p.32, pl.VII) |
| LOCATION | T.62 3.F/6 |
| RN | 70764 |
| DIMENSIONS | 1.9 x 1.4 x 0.9 cm |
| CONDITION | Complete; chips from base, front clypeus and left plate. |
| S. FINISH | No glaze remains. Polished surface. |
| MATERIAL | Steatite. |
| COLOUR | Creamy beige with speckled brown back and sides. |
| DESCRIPTION | Oval shaped scarab seal pierced longitudinally for threading. |
| BACK | Clypeus, head and eyes outlined by single, deep incisions leaving them raised. Large, single incised lines divides head and thorax. Back plain. Wing cases indicated by single incisions on outer edge of back approx. half way down. No internal details. |
| LEGS | Delineated by three incisions. First and uppermost runs from front threading hole to rear. Second and lowest runs from front threading hole, widens midway and then stops approx. two thirds way around side. Third runs diagonally upwards from rear threading hole, to meet the uppermost incision approx. midway along. No feathering attempted. |
| BASE | Oval incised border surrounds design element which can be viewed down length of scarab or across width. Design of either stylised butterfly or a 'cross' design and deeply incised with cross hatching. |

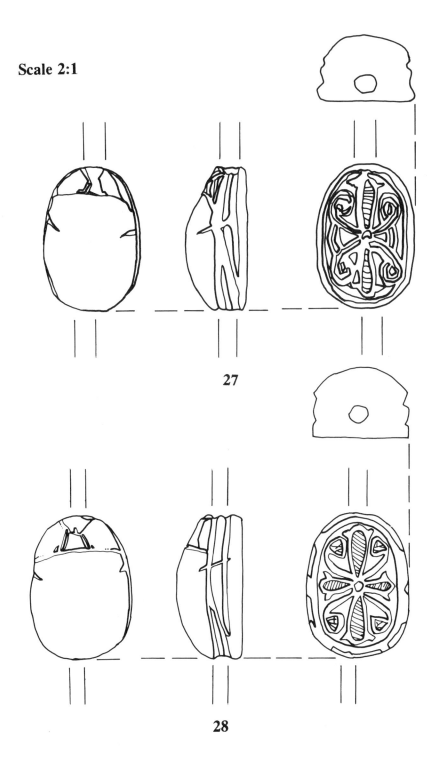

27

28

| | |
|---|---|
| CN | 29 (p.33, pl.VII) |
| LOCATION | T.62 1.D |
| RN | 70406 |
| DIMENSIONS | 1.3 x 0.9 x 0.6 cm |
| CONDITION | Complete. |
| S. FINISH | Surface badly weathered. Blue/green glaze on plates, in leg and base incisions. |
| MATERIAL | Steatite. |
| COLOUR | Orange/beige surface with traces of overlying yellow on back, legs and base incisions. A blue/green glaze on plates and in leg and base incisions overlies the yellow glaze. |
| DESCRIPTION | Oval shaped scarab seal pierced longitudinally for threading. |
| BACK | Clypeus outlined by two single incisions running diagonally back from front edge of plates, meeting behind the head. These lines outline the head and inner edges of stylised eyes. A single incision outlines the outer edge of each eye. Both head and eyes are raised. Single incision divides head and thorax. Back plain. Wing cases indicated by single incisions on outer edge of back approx. half way down. No internal details. |
| LEGS | Delineated by two single incisions running around thickness of scarab from front threading hole to rear. No feathering attempted. |
| BASE | Oval incised border surrounds an incised design. This comprises four concentric circles with a deep, possibly drilled hole in each centre. Circles are linked together by meandering curvilinear line. |

| | |
|---|---|
| CN | 30 (p.33, pl.VII) |
| LOCATION | T.62 3.E |
| RN | 70736 |
| DIMENSIONS | 1.45 x 1.0 x 0.65 cm |
| CONDITION | Complete. |
| S. FINISH | Glaze remains on back and in incisions. |
| MATERIAL | Steatite. |
| COLOUR | Yellow/brown with blue glaze. |
| DESCRIPTION | Oval shaped scarab seal pierced longitudinally for threading. |
| BACK | Clypeus, head and eyes outlined by single incisions leaving them raised. Single incision divides head and thorax. Back plain. Wing cases indicated by single incisions on outer edge of back approx. one third way down. No internal details. |
| LEGS | Delineated by two single incisions running around thickness of scarab from front threading hole to rear. No feathering attempted. |
| BASE | Oval incised border surrounds geometric design. |

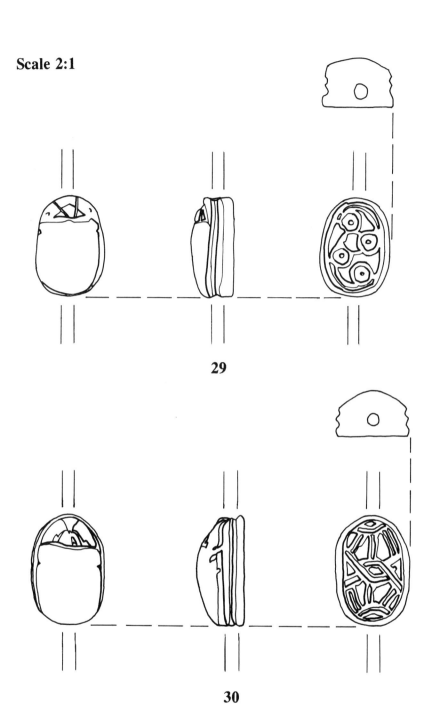

**29**

**30**

| | |
|---|---|
| CN | 31 (p.33, pl. VIII) |
| LOCATION | T.62 3.E/F |
| RN | 70931 |
| DIMENSIONS | 2.35 x 1.6 x 0.85 cm |
| CONDITION | Complete; badly chipped around edge and deep chip on base. |
| S. FINISH | Polished. |
| MATERIAL | Steatite. |
| COLOUR | Yellow/brown. |
| DESCRIPTION | Scaraboid, pierced longitudinally for threading. |
| BACK | No features attempted. Back plain. Threading holes stand out predominantly at each end. |
| LEGS | Delineated by two single incisions running around thickness of scarab from front threading hole to rear. Area between is feathered. |
| BASE | Oval, incised, hatched border surrounds geometric pattern. |


| | |
|---|---|
| CN | 32 (pl. VIII) |
| LOCATION | T.62 1.E |
| RN | 70612 |
| DIMENSIONS | 2.1 x 1.4 x 0.65 cm |
| CONDITION | Complete; one large chip from base. |
| S. FINISH | No glaze remains (except for possible strip down centre of back). Matt surface. |
| MATERIAL | Steatite. |
| COLOUR | Creamy beige. Yellower down centre strip of back. |
| DESCRIPTION | Scaraboid, pierced longitudinally for threading. |
| BACK | Takes appearance of a fish, but with two heads. Each head is styled around the threading hole, which acts as its mouth. The back is covered in 'scales'. |
| LEGS | Not represented. One single incision runs around thickness of scaraboid from front threading hole to rear. No feathering attempted. |
| BASE | Oval incised border surrounds incised pattern. |

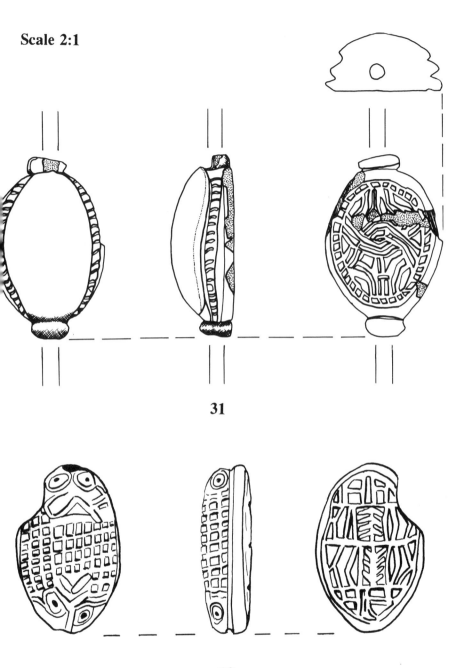

**31**

**32**

| CN | 33 (p.35, pl.VIII) |
|---|---|
| LOCATION | T.62 1.G |
| RN | 70570 |
| DIMENSIONS | 1.5 x 1.0 x 0.65 cm (Base: 1.45 x 1.0 cm) |
| CONDITION | Complete. |
| S. FINISH | Glaze remains on back and plates. Matt surface. |
| MATERIAL | Steatite. |
| COLOUR | Brown with blue/green glaze. Beige base. |
| DESCRIPTION | Oval shaped scarab seal pierced longitudinally for threading. |
| BACK | Clypeus, edge of plates, in high relief due to removal of plates. No head or eyes. Beginning of back defined by removal of plates. Back plain. Wing cases indicated by single incisions on outer edge of back approx. half way down. No internal details. |
| LEGS | Delineated by two single incisions running around thickness of scarab from front threading hole to rear. No feathering attempted. |
| BASE | Incised, roughly oval border surrounds three motifs: an s-shaped spiral (in reverse) in centre, flanked by a schematized drooping lotus bud. |

| CN | 34 (p.35, pl.VIII) |
|---|---|
| LOCATION | T.62 1.E |
| RN | 70605 |
| DIMENSIONS | 1.5 x 1.1 x 0.6 cm |
| CONDITION | Complete; chips from threading hole at both ends. |
| S. FINISH | Surface worn. No traces of glaze. |
| MATERIAL | Steatite. |
| COLOUR | Beige, a sandy beige on back. |
| DESCRIPTION | Oval shaped scarab seal pierced longitudinally for threading. |
| BACK | Clypeus and head outlined by single incisions. No eyes. Single, deeply incised line divides head and thorax. Back plain. Wing cases indicated by single incisions on outer edge of back approx. half way down. No internal details. |
| LEGS | Delineated by two single incisions running around thickness of scarab from front threading hole to rear. No feathering attempted. |
| BASE | Incised oval border surrounds three panels of incised hieroglyphs: top panel consists of inverted lotus flower with five panels. Middle panel has three large $šn$ signs while bottom panel is a $nb$ sign. |

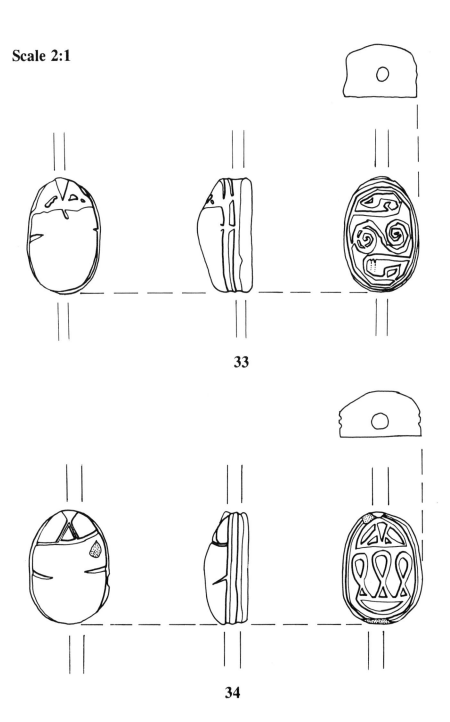

33

34

113

| | |
|---|---|
| CN | 35 (p.36, pl.IX) |
| LOCATION | T.62 1.1 |
| RN | 70665 |
| DIMENSIONS | 1.45 x 1.0 x 0.65 cm |
| CONDITION | Complete. |
| S. FINISH | Surface badly worn. Traces of irridescent glaze in crevices and over wing case. |
| MATERIAL | Steatite. |
| COLOUR | Dull matt yellow/brown surface on off white core. |
| DESCRIPTION | Oval shaped scarab seal pierced longitudinally for threading. |
| BACK | Highly schematic. Single incised lines used to delineate clypeus, head and thorax. Wing cases indicated by single incisions on outer edge of back approx. half way down. No internal details. |
| LEGS | Delineated by two very roughly and deeply incised lines around thickness of scarab. Lines end before reaching front and rear threading holes. A third small incision runs between the two main incisions from rear threading hole. No feathering attempted. |
| BASE | Incised oval border surrounds hieroglyphic design down length of scarab. Design comprised from top: double papyri on side, two ${}^{c}n\underline{h}$ signs flanking $nfr$ signs in centre. Single $r$ or $nb$ sign filling bases of oval. |

| | |
|---|---|
| CN | 36 (p.36, pl.IX) |
| LOCATION | T.62 3.G |
| RN | 70873 |
| DIMENSIONS | 1.65 x 1.2 x 0.75 cm (Base: 1.55 x 1.1 cm) |
| CONDITION | Complete; chips from side near base and head. |
| S. FINISH | Matt surface. |
| MATERIAL | Steatite. |
| COLOUR | Pale beige with brown patches down middle of back, in leg incisions and on base. |
| DESCRIPTION | Oval shaped scarab seal pierced longitudinally for threading. |
| BACK | Clypeus and head outlined by single incision leaving them raised. Single incision outlines eyes and divides head and thorax. Wing cases indicated by single incisions on outer edge of back approx. half way down. No internal details. |
| LEGS | Delineated by two single incisions running around thickness of scarab from front threading hole to rear. No feathering attempted. |
| BASE | Oval incised border surrounds scroll design with wilting papyri on side above. |

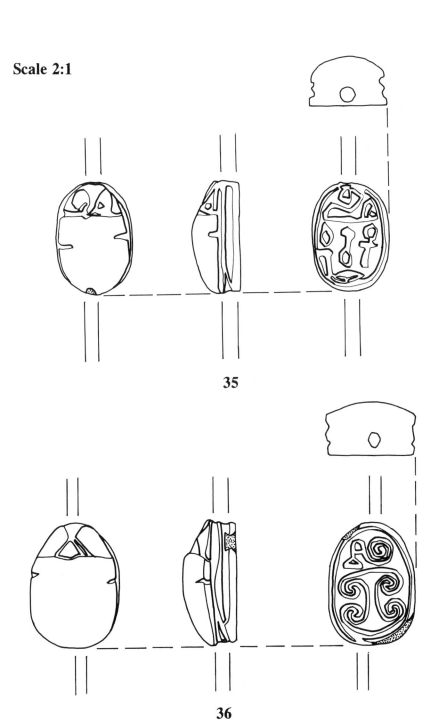

35

36

| | |
|---|---|
| CN | 37 (p.35, pl.IX) |
| LOCATION | T.62 3.1 |
| RN | 70929 |
| DIMENSIONS | 1.5 x 1.0 x 0.7 cm |
| CONDITION | Complete; break from front threading hole. |
| S. FINISH | Matt surface. |
| MATERIAL | Steatite. |
| COLOUR | Beige. Darker and lighter patches on back and head. Light beige in incisions. |
| DESCRIPTION | Oval shaped scarab seal pierced longitudinally for threading. |
| BACK | Head and eyes outlined by single incisions. No clypeus remains. Deeply incised line divides head and thorax. Back plain. Wing cases indicated by single incisions on outer edge of back approx. one third way down. No internal details. |
| LEGS | Delineated by three incisions. First and uppermost runs from front threading hole to rear. Second and lower runs from front threading hole approx. two thirds way around side. Third and lowest runs from the rear threading hole approx. one third way around on same level as second incision. Middle section of middle leg is feathered. |
| BASE | Incised oval border surrounds hieroglyphs arranged down length of scarab. A $w\underline{d}\jmath$ eye and an $\ulcorner nh$ sign within a cartouche are flanked by papyri and an indistinguishable hieroglyph. |

| | |
|---|---|
| CN | 38 (p.37, pl.IX) |
| LOCATION | T.62 3.1 |
| RN | 70933 |
| DIMENSIONS | 1.65 x 1.15 x 0.75 cm |
| CONDITION | Complete; chipped on base. |
| S. FINISH | Surface slightly weathered, possibly 'polished' from handling. |
| MATERIAL | Steatite. |
| COLOUR | Grey with beige base. |
| DESCRIPTION | Oval shaped scarab seal pierced longitudinally for threading. |
| BACK | Clypeus and head outlined by single incisions leaving them raised. Eyes possibly indicated. Single incision divides head and thorax. Back plain. Wing cases indicated by single incisions on outer edge of back approx. one third way down. No internal details. |
| LEGS | Delineated by three incisions. First and uppermost runs from front threading hole to rear. Second and lowest runs from front threading hole approx. two thirds way around side. Third runs from rear threading hole slightly diagonally, approx. one fifth way around, above lowest incision. Feathering at front and rear: RF:8; LF:7; RR:8; LR:9. |
| BASE | Oval incised border surrounds design running across length of scarab. Incised scroll interlocking border surrounds a *nbw* sign. |

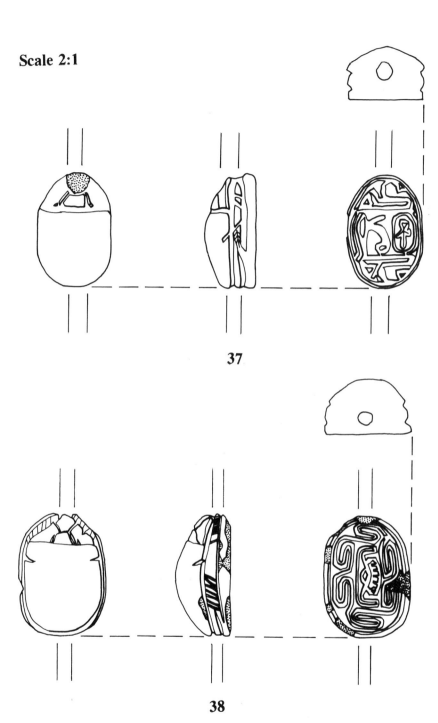

37

38

| CN | 39 (p.37, pl.IX) |
|---|---|
| LOCATION | T.62 3.E |
| RN | 70934 |
| DIMENSIONS | 1.35 x 0.95 x 0.7 cm |
| CONDITION | Complete; large chip from front of scarab, head and clypeus missing. |
| S. FINISH | Light blue powdery glaze remains on sides and base. Matt surface. |
| MATERIAL | Steatite. |
| COLOUR | Brown with blue glaze. |
| DESCRIPTION | Oval shaped scarab seal pierced longitudinally for threading. |
| BACK | Clypeus missing. Very faint incisions outline back of head that remains. Back plain. No indication of wing cases. |
| LEGS | Delineated by extremely faint incisions. One incision runs along top of side, the other along the base. Half way along there is a diagonal incision, and from that incision to the front of the scarab runs another horizontal incision. No feathering attempted. |
| BASE | Oval incised border surrounds design field that runs down length of scarab. Design comprises interlocking spirals, with one vertical incision on body. |

| CN | 40 (p.37, pl.X) |
|---|---|
| LOCATION | T.62 |
| RN | 70975 |
| DIMENSIONS | 1.2 x 0.8 x 0.6 cm (Base: 1.1 x 0.8 cm) |
| CONDITION | Complete; chip from top of threading hole. |
| S. FINISH | Matt surface. |
| MATERIAL | Steatite. |
| COLOUR | Browny beige; light beige on base. |
| DESCRIPTION | Oval shaped scarab seal pierced longitudinally for threading. |
| BACK | Clypeus and head outlined by faint incisions leaving them raised. No eyes indicated. Horn marked. Faint incision divides head and thorax. Back high and plain. Wing cases indicated by single incisions on outer edge of back approx. half way down. No internal details. |
| LEGS | Delineated by two faint, single incisions running around thickness of scarab from front threading hole to rear. No feathering attempted. |
| BASE | Incised oval border surrounds hieroglyph design across length of scarab. A $w_3\underline{d}$ papyrus column in middle is flanked by two other papyri, one wilting on either side. |

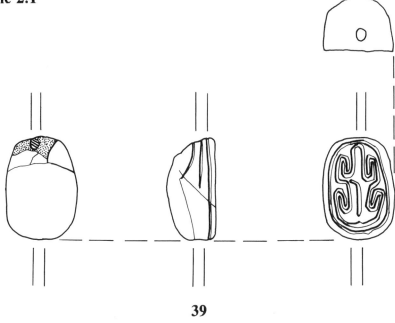

**39**

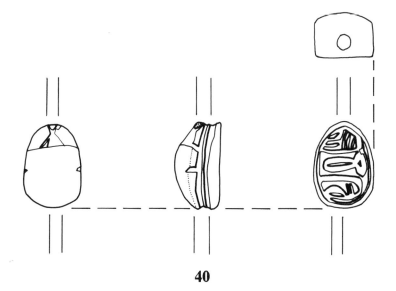

**40**

| | |
|---|---|
| CN | 41 (p.37, pl.X) |
| LOCATION | T.62 1.2 |
| RN | 70291 |
| DIMENSIONS | 1.9 x 1.2 x 0.7 cm |
| CONDITION | Complete; chips from sides and base. |
| S. FINISH | Remains of pearl coloured glaze on clypeus, left side of back, legs, and in $w_3d$ incision on base. Base polished; back and head with matt surface. |
| MATERIAL | Faience (?). |
| COLOUR | Beige. Yellow in incision right side of clypeus and within breaks of front legs on RHS. Base chip interior is pink. |
| DESCRIPTION | Oval shaped scarab seal pierced longitudinally for threading. |
| BACK | Clypeus and head outlined by single incisions leaving them raised. Eyes incised on top of clypeus. Single incision divides head and thorax. Back plain. Wing cases indicated by single incisions on outer edge of back approx. half way down. No internal details. |
| LEGS | Delineated by three incisions. First and uppermost runs from front threading hole to rear. Second and lowest runs from front threading hole approx. two thirds way around side. Third runs from rear threading hole, in between first two incisions approx one third way around side. Middle section and back legs are feathered. |
| BASE | Oval border surrounds hieroglyphs arranged in four panels down length of scarab. At top, a $w_3d$ is flanked by two *horus* flacons; underneath two $wd_3t$ eyes, then a *ḫpr* beetle flanked by two *ʿnḫ*'s in ovals on top of a *nbw*. |

| | |
|---|---|
| CN | 42 (p.36, pl.X) |
| LOCATION | T.62 3.G |
| RN | 70874 |
| DIMENSIONS | 1.9 x 1.2 x 0.6 cm (Base: 1.8 x 1.15 cm) |
| CONDITION | Complete; but chipped. |
| S. FINISH | Badly weathered and uneven, cracked. Matt surface. |
| MATERIAL | Bone/ivory. |
| COLOUR | Beige. |
| DESCRIPTION | Scaraboid, pierced longitudinally for threading. |
| BACK | Plain, no features attempted. |
| LEGS | Delineated by two single incisions running around thickness of scarab from front threading hole to rear. Area between incisions is feathered. |
| BASE | Oval incised border surrounds hieroglyph design running across length of scarab. Two crowns of Upper/Lower Egypt take up outside positions. Between them, from top to bottom: two *nfr* signs with *ʿnḫ* between; below two *ʿnḫ*'s with a *nfr* in between, over a *nb* or *r* sign. |

120

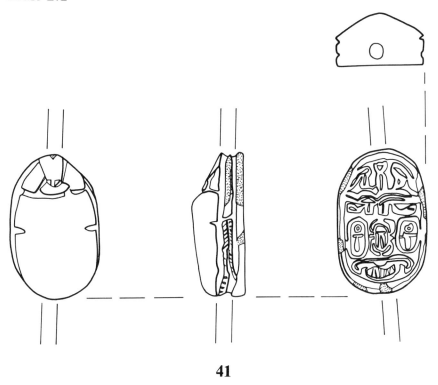

**41**

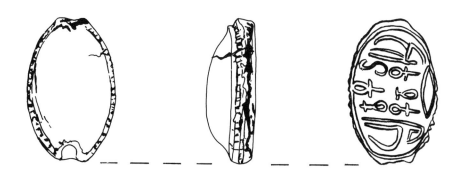

**42**

| | |
|---|---|
| CN | 43 (p.38, pl.X) |
| LOCATION | T.62 3.G |
| RN | 70876 |
| DIMENSIONS | 2.0 x 1.4 x 0.95 cm |
| CONDITION | Complete; chips on sides and base. No glaze remains. |
| S. FINISH | Matt finish. |
| MATERIAL | Steatite. |
| COLOUR | Yellow/brown. |
| DESCRIPTION | Oval shaped scarab seal pierced longitudinally for threading. |
| BACK | Clypeus, head and plates outlined by single incisions. Single incision divides head and thorax. Wing case represented by faint incision on outer edge of left side approx. one third way down. No internal details. |
| LEGS | Delineated by three incisions. First and uppermost runs from front threading hole to rear. Second and lowest runs from front threading hole, widens midway and stops approx. two thirds way around side. Third runs diagonally upwards from rear threading hole to meet uppermost incision approx. midway along. Legs are feathered and notched at front. |
| BASE | Oval incised border surrounds hieroglyhs arranged in a random order and not in the same direction. They include: $k_3$, Hr, r, n, $wd_3t$, nbw. |

| | |
|---|---|
| CN | 44 (p.38, pl.X) |
| LOCATION | T.62 3.1 |
| RN | 70879 |
| DIMENSIONS | 1.5 x 1.0 x 0.6 cm |
| CONDITION | Complete; large chip from front left. |
| S. FINISH | Weathered surface |
| MATERIAL | Steatite. |
| COLOUR | Beige, with darker patches. |
| DESCRIPTION | Oval shaped scarab seal pierced longitudinally for threading. |
| BACK | Clypeus and part of head and eyes missing. RHS of head outlined faintly by an incision and raised. Single, faint incision divides head and thorax. Back plain. Wing cases indicated by single incisions on outer edge of back approx. half way down. No internal details. Threading hole does not reach from back to front. |
| LEGS | Delineated by three incisions. First and uppermost runs from front threading hole to rear. Second and lowest runs from front threading hole, widens midway and then stops approx. four fifths way around side. Third runs diagonally upwards from rear threading hole to meet uppermost incision approx. one third way around. No feathering attempted. |
| BASE | Faintly incised oval border surrounds hieroglyphs running down length of scarab. From top: double ʿnh flanked by ureai; $k_3$ flanked by Hr falcons, then nfr flanked by ʿnh and $w_3d$'s, on nb or r. |

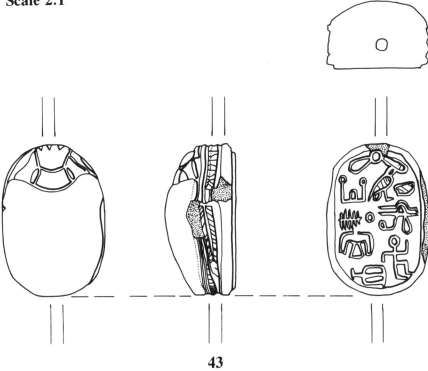

**43**

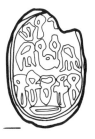

**44**

| | |
|---|---|
| CN | 45 (p.38, pl.XI) |
| LOCATION | T.62 4.D |
| RN | 70927 |
| DIMENSIONS | 2.0 x 1.35 x 0.75 cm |
| CONDITION | Complete; chips from base, front threading hole and clypeus. |
| S. FINISH | Slightly weathered. Very small amounts of glaze remains in incisions on base. |
| MATERIAL | Steatite. |
| COLOUR | Off–white. |
| DESCRIPTION | Oval shaped scarab seal pierced longitudinally for threading. |
| BACK | Clypeus, head and eyes outlined by single incisions leaving them raised. Single incision divides head and thorax. Back plain. Wing cases indicated by single incisions on outer edge of back approx. half way down. No internal details. |
| LEGS | Delineated by two single incisions running around thickness of scarab from front threading hole to rear. Lowest incision runs approx. two thirds way around side before lifting slightly to continue to rear threading hole. Area in between is feathered in front and back. |
| BASE | Oval incised border surrounds design. This comprises random hieroglyphs surrounded by a looped scroll border. |

| | |
|---|---|
| CN | 46 (p.39, pl.XI) |
| LOCATION | T.62 1.G |
| RN | 70520 |
| DIMENSIONS | 1.7 x 1.4 x 0.45 cm |
| CONDITION | Complete; chips on base around front and rear threading holes. |
| S. FINISH | Matt finish. |
| MATERIAL | Steatite. |
| COLOUR | Beige/brown. |
| DESCRIPTION | Scaraboid pierced longitudinally for threading. |
| BACK | Plain, no attempt at details. |
| LEGS | One single incision runs around side of scaraboid. No feathering attempted. |
| BASE | Roundish incised 'rope' border surrounds design running down length of scaraboid. Design comprises hieroglyphs standing on a horizontal line. In the middle are two *sn* signs, flanked by a standing and wilting papyri. Above the *šn* signs is an *nb* sign. Below the horizontal (incised) line is a second, and below that two paris of double incised lines cut in a 'v' shape. |

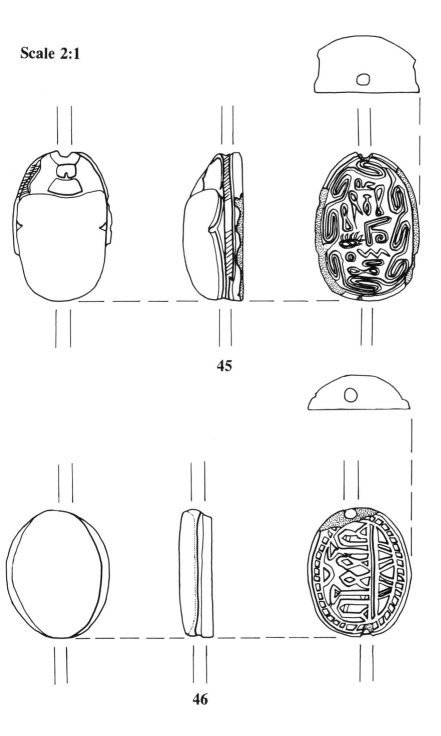

45

46

| | |
|---|---|
| CN | 47 (p.39, pl.XI) |
| LOCATION | T.62 3.H/I |
| RN | 70875 |
| DIMENSIONS | 1.75 x 1.25 x 0.85 cm |
| CONDITION | Complete; chipped at base at rear. |
| S. FINISH | Glaze remains on plates, legs and in base incisions. |
| MATERIAL | Steatite. |
| COLOUR | Brown with blue/green glaze. |
| DESCRIPTION | Oval shaped scarab seal pierced longitudinally for threading. |
| BACK | Clypeus and eyes outlined by single incisions leaving them raised. No head represented. Single incision divides head and thorax. Back plain. Wing cases indicated by single incisions on outer edge of back approx. half way down. No internal details. |
| LEGS | Delineated by two single incisions running around thickness of scarab from front threading hole to rear. No feathering attempted. |
| BASE | Oval incised border surrounds hieroglyphs running across length of scarab. Two *šn* signs flanked by two papyri stand on two incised lines with vertical hatching in the centre. A *nb* sign lies above the *šn*. |

| | |
|---|---|
| CN | 48 (p.39, pl.XI) |
| LOCATION | T.62 3.E |
| RN | 70930 |
| DIMENSIONS | 1.75 x 1.25 x 0.9 cm |
| CONDITION | Complete. |
| S. FINISH | Surface worn. |
| MATERIAL | Steatite. |
| COLOUR | Dull brown/beige. Dark brown patches on back, side and head. Pale core. Remains of whitish, pasty substance in incisions, with 'sheen' in areas. |
| DESCRIPTION | Oval shaped scarab seal pierced longitudinally for threading. |
| BACK | Clypeus, head and eyes outlined by single incisions. Single incision divides head and thorax. Back plain. Wing cases indicated by single incisions on outer edge of back approx. half way down. No internal details. |
| LEGS | Delineated by three shallow incisions. First and uppermost runs from front threading hole to rear. Second and lowest runs from front threading hole approx. two thirds way around side. Third runs from rear threading hole, on same level as second incision but stops before they join. No attempt at feathering. |
| BASE | Incised oval border surrounds hieroglyphic design which runs across length of scarab. Ground line supports two *šn* signs in the centre flanked by a pair of plant motifs, one standing vertically, the outer wilting. Between ground line and border is filled with slightly curved line with vertical nicks. Above whole design is a *nb* shaped sign. |

Scale 2:1

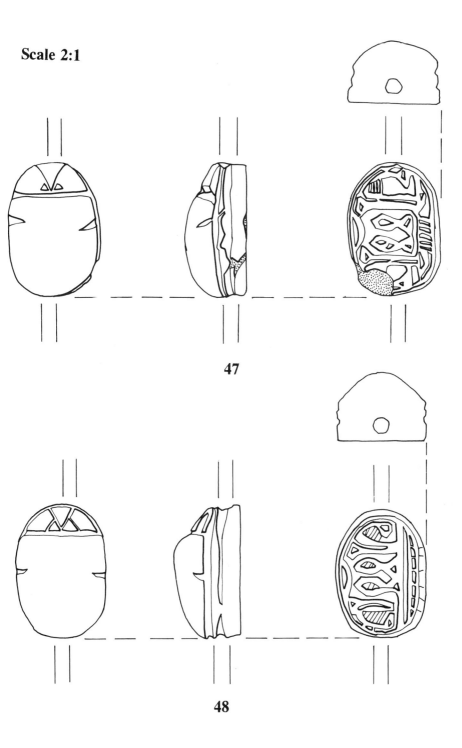

47

48

| CN | 49 (p.5, pl.XII) |
|---|---|
| LOCATION | T.62 1.F |
| RN | 70871 |
| DIMENSIONS | 1.3 x 0.85 x 0.6 cm |
| CONDITION | Complete. |
| S. FINISH | Surface weathered. Patches of glaze cover all scarab. |
| MATERIAL | Faience. |
| COLOUR | Glaze is light blue/green underlay with patches of darker blue and green. |
| DESCRIPTION | Oval shaped scarab seal pierced longitudinally for threading. |
| BACK | Clypeus, right eye and front edge of plates and head outlined by single incisions leaving them raised above low relief plates. Removal of plates creates division with back. Back plain. Wing cases indicated by single incisions on outer edge of back approx. two thirds way down. No internal details. |
| LEGS | Delineated by two single incisions running around thickness of scarab from front threading hole to rear. Top right line does not meet threading hole at front. No feathering attempted. |
| BASE | Design can be read either across or down length of scarab and comprises of two winged *horus'* facing inwards with an *r* in middle. |

| CN | 50 (p.5, pl.XII) |
|---|---|
| LOCATION | T.62 2.G |
| RN | 70872 |
| DIMENSIONS | 1.25 x 0.8 x 0.65 cm |
| CONDITION | Complete. |
| S. FINISH | Extremely worn. Traces of glaze on plates. |
| MATERIAL | Faience. |
| COLOUR | White with remains of green glaze on plates and outer edge of back and sides. |
| DESCRIPTION | Oval shaped scarab seal pierced longitudinally for threading. |
| BACK | Clypeus, head and eyes are indistinguishable. Slightly raised area indicates their area. Very shallow incision divides head and thorax. Back plain. One wing case on LHS indicated by an incision on outer edge of back approx. half way down. No internal details. |
| LEGS | Delineated by two shallow and hardly perceptible incision running around thickness of scarab, from front threading hole to rear. No feathering attempted. |
| BASE | Design is indistinguishable. No border. Design might comprise three sections which could represent some sort of hieroglyph. |

128

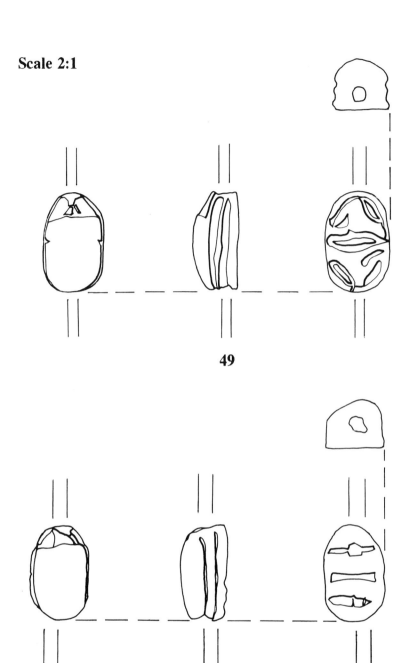

49

50

| CN | 51 (p.5, pl.XII) |
|---|---|
| LOCATION | T.62 3.E |
| RN | 70932 |
| DIMENSIONS | 1.2 x 0.85 x 0.6 cm |
| CONDITION | Complete; chip from front threading hole. |
| S. FINISH | Extremely worn fabric with traces of green glaze. |
| MATERIAL | Faience. |
| COLOUR | Beige with white patches on head and back. Remains of green glaze on back, sides and base. |
| DESCRIPTION | Oval shaped scarab seal pierced longitudinally for threading. |
| BACK | No details of head distinguishable. Probably shallow incision divides head and thorax. Back plain. Possible wing cases indicated by faint markings on outer edge of back approx. half way down. No internal details. |
| LEGS | Delineated by a single incision running around thickness of scarab from front threading hole to rear. No feathering attempted. |
| BASE | Impossible to distinguish details, but probable design did exist. |

| CN | 52 (p.7, pl.XII) |
|---|---|
| LOCATION | T.62 1.G |
| RN | 70542 |
| DIMENSIONS | 1.9 x 1.3 x 0.9 cm |
| CONDITION | Complete; chips from side and base. |
| S. FINISH | Polished. |
| MATERIAL | Amethyst |
| COLOUR | Translucent purple. |
| DESCRIPTION | Oval shaped scarab seal pierced longitudinally for threading. |
| BACK | Clypeus, head and eyes outlined by single incisions. Clypeus has three notches at front. Single incision divides head and prothorax, and another incision separates prothorax and elytra. A single incision running perpendicular to this line divides the elytra into two. Wing cases assimilated with incision dividing prothorax and elytra. |
| LEGS | Delineated by a series of incisions running from front threading hole to rear. The uppermost and lowest incisions run from front threading hole to rear. A third incision runs from front threading hole approx. two thirds way around side. Two incisions run diagonally parallel from rear threading hole to meet uppermost line. No feathering attempted. |
| BASE | Plain. |

**Scale 2:1**

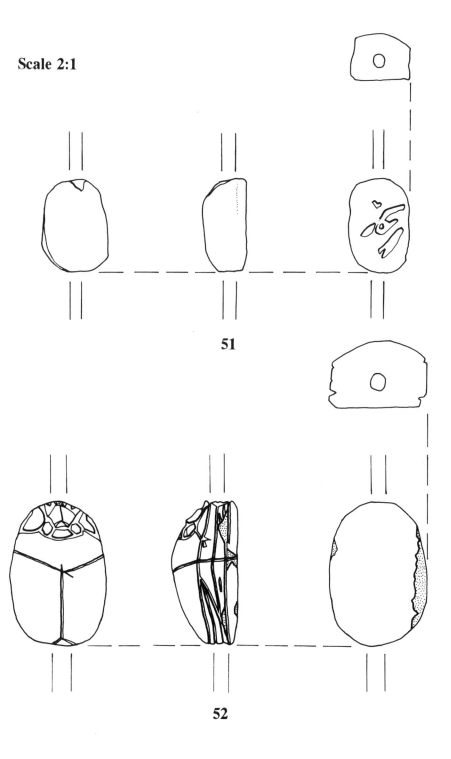

51

52

| CN | 53 (p.5 (n.13), pl.XII) |
|---|---|
| LOCATION | T.62 1.G |
| RN | 70543 |
| DIMENSIONS | 1.9 x 1.3 x 1.0 cm |
| CONDITION | Complete; chips from base, side at front and large chip from left side near rear. |
| S. FINISH | Blistered. Scarab has been burnt and material is very friable. |
| MATERIAL | Faience |
| COLOUR | Totally discoloured, probably by burning. Now a mother of pearl sheen with a mustard coloured streak on the back and small charcoal coloured patches from burning. |
| DESCRIPTION | Oval shaped scarab seal pierced longitudinally for threading. |
| BACK | Details difficult to distinguish. Shallow impressions outline head and clypeus. Horizontal lines arc impressed across the back, with five impressed vertical lines attached to the lowest horizontal line. These run perpendicular to the lower half of the back. Wing cases therefore not represented. |
| LEGS | No attempt to depict legs, or feathering. |
| BASE | Flat and undecorated. |

| CN | 54 (p.8, pl.XIII) |
|---|---|
| LOCATION | T.62 1.G |
| RN | 70607 |
| DIMENSIONS | 1.6 x 1.15 x 0.8 cm |
| CONDITION | Intact. |
| S. FINISH | Polished (perhaps naturally). |
| MATERIAL | Enstatite. |
| COLOUR | Pale greeny/beige stone with a network of tiny, dark (blue/grey) veins. |
| DESCRIPTION | Oval shaped scarab seal pierced longitudinally for threading. |
| BACK | No attempt to delineate features except between head region and back, the latter being higher than the former. One small drilled hole lies above the front threading hole, and meets intended threading hole through scarab body. |
| LEGS | Delineated by three incisions. On the LHS three incisions have been cut into the stone. The two top incisions run slightly diagonally; they do not extend as far as the threading holes. The third, lower incision runs to a small triangle in the middle to delineate the legs. On the RHS three very faint incisions delineate the legs; two horizontal lines the tops of the legs and the third, diagonal line indicates the back leg. No feathering attempted. |
| BASE | Extremely faint incisions perhaps indicate a design on one half of the scarab split onto two groups. A small depression diagonally across the base appears to be a natural flaw in the stone. |

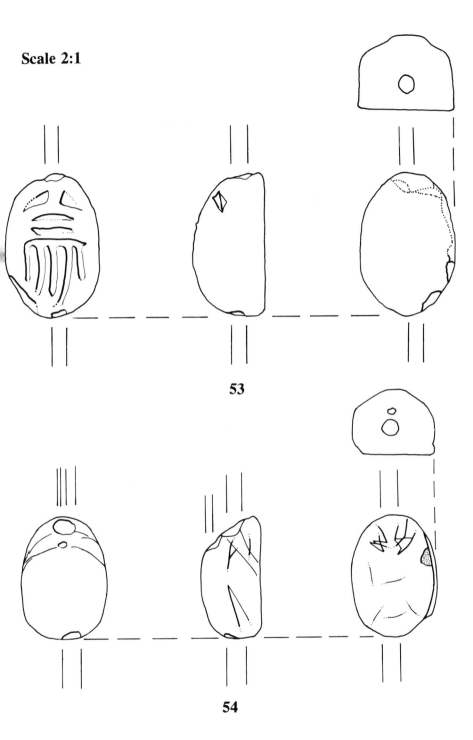

53

54

| | |
|---|---|
| CN | 55 (p.8, pl.XIII) |
| LOCATION | T.62 3.D |
| RN | 70758 |
| DIMENSIONS | 2.05 x 1.6 x 1.0 cm |
| CONDITION | Complete; badly cracked on back, particularly around rear threading hole and on right side. Two depressions on either side of base. |
| S. FINISH | Petrified/ burnt. |
| MATERIAL | Wood. |
| COLOUR | Brown. |
| DESCRIPTION | Oval shaped scarab seal pierced longitudinally for threading. |
| BACK | No details attempted except depressions in head area to indicate eyes, leaving clypeus and head raised. Back plain. No wing cases attempted. |
| LEGS | No attempt has been made to indicate legs. |
| BASE | No visible design or working on base, although two depressions exist. |

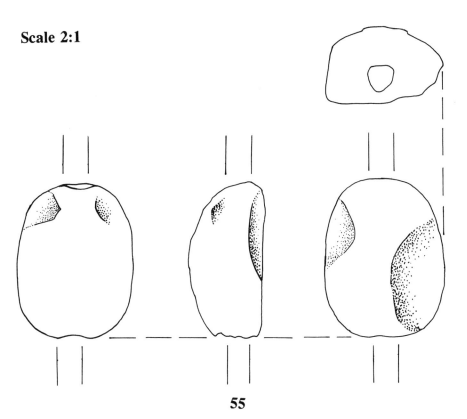

55

# REFERENCE TO PLATES

## Reference to plates cont'd

# PLATES

PLATE I

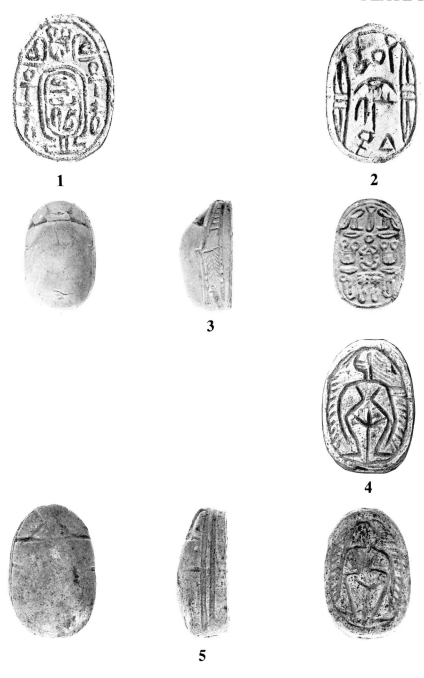

1

2

3

4

5

**Scale 2:1**

**PLATE II**

6

7

8

9

Scale 2:1

PLATE III

10

11

12

13

Scale 2:1

PLATE IV

**14**

**15**

**16**

**17**

Scale 2:1

PLATE V

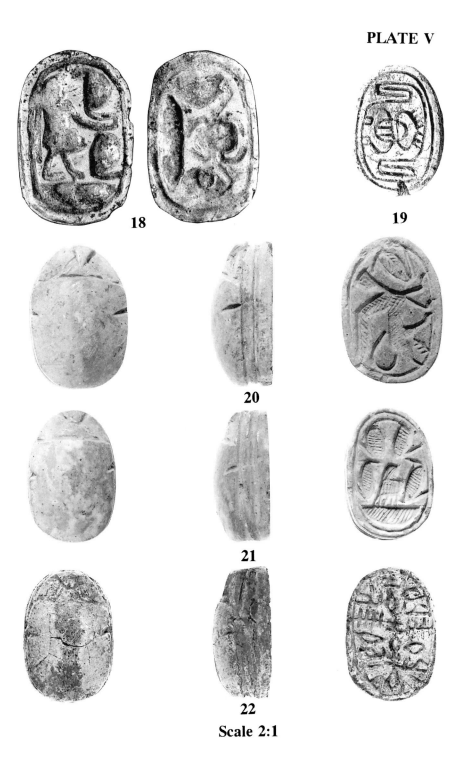

18

19

20

21

22

Scale 2:1

PLATE VI

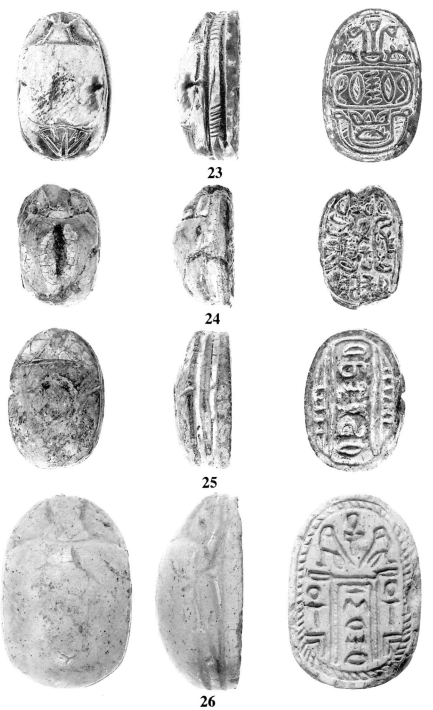

**23**

**24**

**25**

**26**

**Scale 2:1**

**PLATE VII**

**27**

**28**

**29**

**30**

**Scale 2:1**

**PLATE VIII**

**31**

**32**

**33**

**34**

**Scale 2:1**

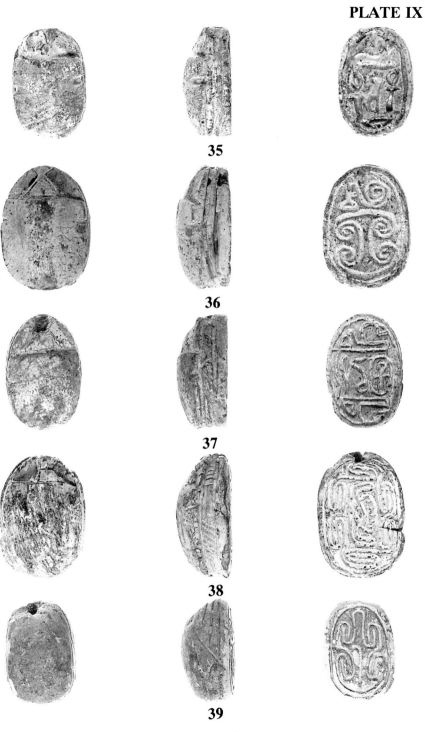

PLATE IX

35

36

37

38

39

Scale 2:1

PLATE X

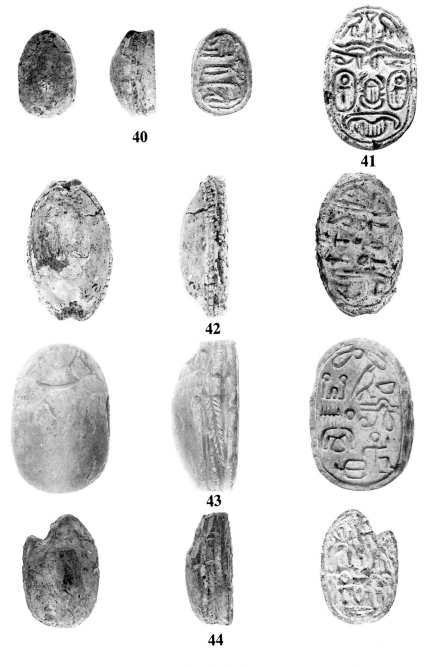

40

41

42

43

44

Scale 2:1

PLATE XI

45

46

47

48

Scale 2:1

PLATE XII

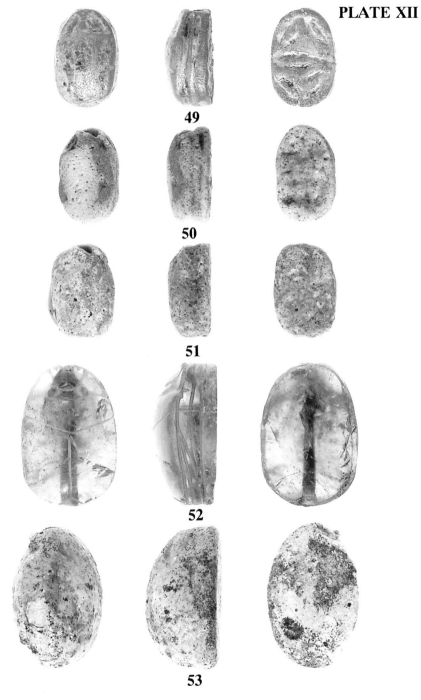

49

50

51

52

53

Scale 2:1

PLATE XIII

54

55

56

Scale 2:1

ORBIS BIBLICUS ET ORIENTALIS

Bd. 19    MASSÉO CALOZ: *Etude sur la LXX origénienne du Psautier.* Les relations entre les leçons des Psaumes du Manuscrit Coislin 44, les Fragments des Hexaples et le texte du Psautier Gallican. 480 pages. 1978.

Bd. 20    RAPHAEL GIVEON: *The Impact of Egypt on Canaan.* Iconographical and Related Studies. 156 Seiten, 73 Abbildungen. 1978.

Bd. 21    DOMINIQUE BARTHÉLEMY: *Etudes d'histoire du texte de l'Ancien Testament.* XXV–419 pages. 1978. Epuisé.

Bd. 22/1  CESLAS SPICQ: *Notes de Lexicographie néo-testamentaire.* Tome I: p. 1–524. 1978. Epuisé.

Bd. 22/2  CESLAS SPICQ: *Notes de Lexicographie néo-testamentaire.* Tome II: p. 525–980. 1978. Epuisé.

Bd. 22/3  CESLAS SPICQ: *Notes de Lexicographie néo-testamentaire.* Supplément. 698 pages. 1982.

Bd. 23    BRIAN M. NOLAN: *The Royal Son of God.* The Christology of Matthew 1–2 in the Setting of the Gospel. 282 Seiten. 1979. Out of print.

Bd. 24    KLAUS KIESOW: *Exodustexte im Jesajabuch.* Literarkritische und motivgeschichtliche Analysen. 221 Seiten. 1979. Vergriffen.

Bd. 25/1  MICHAEL LATTKE: *Die Oden Salomos in ihrer Bedeutung für Neues Testament und Gnosis.* Band I. Ausführliche Handschriftenbeschreibung. Edition mit deutscher Parallel-Übersetzung. Hermeneutischer Anhang zur gnostischen Interpretation der Oden Salomos in der Pistis Sophia. XI–237 Seiten. 1979.

Bd. 25/1a MICHAEL LATTKE: *Die Oden Salomos in ihrer Bedeutung für Neues Testament und Gnosis.* Band Ia. Der syrische Text der Edition in Estrangela Faksimile des griechischen Papyrus Bodmer XI. 68 Seiten. 1980.

Bd. 25/2  MICHAEL LATTKE: *Die Oden Salomos in ihrer Bedeutung für Neues Testament und Gnosis.* Band II. Vollständige Wortkonkordanz zur handschriftlichen, griechischen, koptischen, lateinischen und syrischen Überlieferung der Oden Salomos. Mit einem Faksimile des Kodex N. XVI–201 Seiten. 1979.

Bd. 25/3  MICHAEL LATTKE: *Die Oden Salomos in ihrer Bedeutung für Neues Testament und Gnosis.* Band III. XXXIV–478 Seiten. 1986.

Bd. 26    MAX KÜCHLER: *Frühjüdische Weisheitstraditionen.* Zum Fortgang weisheitlichen Denkens im Bereich des frühjüdischen Jahweglaubens. 703 Seiten. 1979. Vergriffen.

Bd. 27    JOSEF M. OESCH: *Petucha und Setuma.* Untersuchungen zu einer überlieferten Gliederung im hebräischen Text des Alten Testaments. XX–392–37* Seiten. 1979.

Bd. 28    ERIK HORNUNG / OTHMAR KEEL (Herausgeber): *Studien zu altägyptischen Lebenslehren.* 394 Seiten. 1979.

Bd. 29    HERMANN ALEXANDER SCHLÖGL: *Der Gott Tatenen.* Nach Texten und Bildern des Neuen Reiches. 216 Seiten, 14 Abbildungen. 1980.

Bd. 30    JOHANN JAKOB STAMM: *Beiträge zur Hebräischen und Altorientalischen Namenkunde.* XVI–264 Seiten. 1980.

Bd. 31    HELMUT UTZSCHNEIDER: *Hosea – Prophet vor dem Ende.* Zum Verhältnis von Geschichte und Institution in der alttestamentlichen Prophetie. 260 Seiten. 1980.

Bd. 32    PETER WEIMAR: *Die Berufung des Mose.* Literaturwissenschaftliche Analyse von Exodus 2, 23–5, 5. 402 Seiten. 1980.

Bd. 33    OTHMAR KEEL: *Das Böcklein in der Milch seiner Mutter und Verwandtes.* Im Lichte eines altorientalischen Bildmotivs. 163 Seiten, 141 Abbildungen. 1980.

Bd. 34    PIERRE AUFFRET: *Hymnes d'Egypte et d'Israël.* Etudes de structures littéraires. 316 pages, 1 illustration. 1981.

Bd. 35    ARIE VAN DER KOOIJ: *Die alten Textzeugen des Jesajabuches.* Ein Beitrag zur Textgeschichte des Alten Testaments. 388 Seiten. 1981.

Bd. 36    CARMEL McCARTHY: *The Tiqqune Sopherim and Other Theological Corrections in the Masoretic Text of the Old Testament.* 280 Seiten. 1981.

Bd. 37    BARBARA L. BEGELSBACHER-FISCHER: *Untersuchungen zur Götterwelt des Alten Reiches im Spiegel der Privatgräber der IV. und V. Dynastie.* 336 Seiten. 1981.

Bd. 38    MÉLANGES DOMINIQUE BARTHÉLEMY. *Etudes bibliques offertes à l'occasion de son 60ᵉ anniversaire.* Edités par Pierre Casetti, Othmar Keel et Adrian Schenker. 724 pages, 31 illustrations. 1981.

Bd. 39    ANDRÉ LEMAIRE: *Les écoles et la formation de la Bible dans l'ancien Israël.* 142 pages, 14 illustrations. 1981.

Bd. 40    JOSEPH HENNINGER: *Arabica Sacra.* Aufsätze zur Religionsgeschichte Arabiens und seiner Randgebiete. Contributions à l'histoire religieuse de l'Arabie et de ses régions limitrophes. 347 Seiten. 1981.

Bd. 41    DANIEL VON ALLMEN: *La famille de Dieu.* La symbolique familiale dans le paulinisme. LXVII–330 pages, 27 planches. 1981.

Bd. 42    ADRIAN SCHENKER: *Der Mächtige im Schmelzofen des Mitleids.* Eine Interpretation von 2 Sam 24. 92 Seiten. 1982.

Bd. 43    PAUL DESELAERS: *Das Buch Tobit.* Studien zu seiner Entstehung, Komposition und Theologie. 532 Seiten + Übersetzung 16 Seiten. 1982.

Bd. 44    PIERRE CASETTI: *Gibt es ein Leben vor dem Tod?* Eine Auslegung von Psalm 49. 315 Seiten. 1982.

Bd. 45    FRANK-LOTHAR HOSSFELD: *Der Dekalog.* Seine späten Fassungen, die originale Komposition und seine Vorstufen. 308 Seiten. 1982. Vergriffen.

Bd. 46    ERIK HORNUNG: *Der ägyptische Mythos von der Himmelskuh.* Eine Ätiologie des Unvollkommenen. Unter Mitarbeit von Andreas Brodbeck, Hermann Schlögl und Elisabeth Staehelin und mit einem Beitrag von Gerhard Fecht. XII–129 Seiten, 10 Abbildungen. 1991. 2. ergänzte Auflage.

Bd. 47    PIERRE CHERIX: *Le Concept de Notre Grande Puissance (CG VI, 4).* Texte, remarques philologiques, traduction et notes. XIV–95 pages. 1982.

Bd. 48    JAN ASSMANN / WALTER BURKERT / FRITZ STOLZ: *Funktionen und Leistungen des Mythos.* Drei altorientalische Beispiele. 118 Seiten, 17 Abbildungen. 1982. Vergriffen.

Bd. 49    PIERRE AUFFRET: *La sagesse a bâti sa maison.* Etudes de structures littéraires dans l'Ancien Testament et spécialement dans les psaumes. 580 pages. 1982.

Bd. 50/1  DOMINIQUE BARTHÉLEMY: *Critique textuelle de l'Ancien Testament.* 1. Josué, Juges, Ruth, Samuel, Rois, Chroniques, Esdras, Néhémie, Esther. Rapport final du Comité pour l'analyse textuelle de l'Ancien Testament hébreu institué par l'Alliance Biblique Universelle, établi en coopération avec Alexander R. Hulst †, Norbert Lohfink, William D. McHardy, H. Peter Rüger, coéditeur, James A. Sanders, coéditeur. 812 pages. 1982.

Bd. 67    OTHMAR KEEL / SILVIA SCHROER: *Studien zu den Stempelsiegeln aus Palästina/Israel.* Band I. 115 Seiten, 103 Abbildungen. 1985.

Bd. 68    WALTER BEYERLIN: *Weisheitliche Vergewisserung mit Bezug auf den Zionskult.* Studien zum 125. Psalm. 96 Seiten. 1985.

Bd. 69    RAPHAEL VENTURA: *Living in a City of the Dead.* A Selection of Topographical and Administrative Terms in the Documents of the Theban Necropolis. XII–232 Seiten. 1986.

Bd. 70    CLEMENS LOCHER: *Die Ehre einer Frau in Israel.* Exegetische und rechtsvergleichende Studien zu Dtn 22, 13–21. XVIII–464 Seiten. 1986.

Bd. 71    HANS-PETER MATHYS: *Liebe deinen Nächsten wie dich selbst.* Untersuchungen zum alttestamentlichen Gebot der Nächstenliebe (Lev 19,18). XII–204 Seiten. 1990. 2. verbesserte Auflage.

Bd. 72    FRIEDRICH ABITZ: *Ramses III. in den Gräbern seiner Söhne.* 156 Seiten, 31 Abbildungen. 1986.

Bd. 73    DOMINIQUE BARTHÉLEMY/DAVID W. GOODING/JOHAN LUST/EMANUEL TOV: *The Story of David and Goliath.* 160 Seiten. 1986.

Bd. 74    SILVIA SCHROER: *In Israel gab es Bilder.* Nachrichten von darstellender Kunst im Alten Testament. XVI–553 Seiten, 146 Abbildungen. 1987.

Bd. 75    ALAN R. SCHULMAN: *Ceremonial Execution and Public Rewards.* Some Historical Scenes on New Kingdom Private Stelae. 296 Seiten, 41 Abbildungen. 1987.

Bd. 76    JOŽE KRAŠOVEC: *La justice (Ṣdq) de Dieu dans la Bible hébraïque et l'interprétation juive et chrétienne.* 456 pages. 1988.

Bd. 77    HELMUT UTZSCHNEIDER: *Das Heiligtum und das Gesetz.* Studien zur Bedeutung der sinaitischen Heiligtumstexte (Ez 25–40; Lev 8–9). XIV–326 Seiten. 1988.

Bd. 78    BERNARD GOSSE: *Isaie 13,1–14,23.* Dans la tradition littéraire du livre d'Isaïe et dans la tradition des oracles contre les nations. 308 pages. 1988.

Bd. 79    INKE W. SCHUMACHER: *Der Gott Sopdu – Der Herr der Fremdländer.* XVI–364 Seiten, 6 Abbildungen. 1988.

Bd. 80    HELLMUT BRUNNER: *Das hörende Herz.* Kleine Schriften zur Religions- und Geistesgeschichte Ägyptens. Herausgegeben von Wolfgang Röllig. 449 Seiten, 55 Abbildungen. 1988.

Bd. 81    WALTER BEYERLIN: *Bleilot, Brecheisen oder was sonst?* Revision einer Amos-Vision. 68 Seiten. 1988.

Bd. 82    MANFRED HUTTER: *Behexung, Entsühnung und Heilung.* Das Ritual der Tunnawiya für ein Königspaar aus mittelhethitischer Zeit (KBo XXI 1 – KUB IX 34 – KBo XXI 6). 186 Seiten. 1988.

Bd. 83    RAPHAEL GIVEON: *Scarabs from Recent Excavations in Israel.* 114 Seiten. Mit zahlreichen Abbildungen im Text und 9 Tafeln. 1988.

Bd. 84    MIRIAM LICHTHEIM: *Ancient Egyptian Autobiographies chiefly of the Middle Kingdom.* A Study and an Anthology. 200 Seiten, 10 Seiten Abbildungen. 1988.

Bd. 85    ECKART OTTO: *Rechtsgeschichte der Redaktionen im Kodex Ešnunna und im «Bundesbuch».* Eine redaktionsgeschichtliche und rechtsvergleichende Studie zu altbabylonischen und altisraelitischen Rechtsüberlieferungen. 220 Seiten. 1989.

Bd. 86    ANDRZEJ NIWIŃSKI: *Studies on the Illustrated Theban Funerary Papyri of the 11th and 10th Centuries B.C.* 488 Seiten, 80 Seiten Tafeln. 1989.

Bd. 87    URSULA SEIDL: *Die babylonischen Kudurru-Reliefs.* Symbole mesopotamischer Gottheiten. 236 Seiten, 33 Tafeln und 2 Tabellen. 1989.

Bd. 88 OTHMAR KEEL / HILDI KEEL-LEU / SILVIA SCHROER: *Studien zu den Stempelsiegeln aus Palästina / Israel.* Band II. 364 Seiten, 652 Abbildungen. 1989.

Bd. 89 FRIEDRICH ABITZ: *Baugeschichte und Dekoration des Grabes Ramses' VI.* 202 Seiten, 39 Abbildungen. 1989.

Bd. 90 JOSEPH HENNINGER SVD: *Arabica varia.* Aufsätze zur Kulturgeschichte Arabiens und seiner Randgebiete. Contributions à l'histoire culturelle de l'Arabie et de ses régions limitrophes. 504 Seiten. 1989.

Bd. 91 GEORG FISCHER: *Jahwe unser Gott.* Sprache, Aufbau und Erzähltechnik in der Berufung des Mose (Ex. 3–4). 276 Seiten. 1989.

Bd. 92 MARK A. O'BRIEN: *The Deuteronomistic History Hypothesis:* A Reassessment. 340 Seiten. 1989.

Bd. 93 WALTER BEYERLIN: *Reflexe der Amosvisionen im Jeremiabuch.* 120 Seiten. 1989.

Bd. 94 ENZO CORTESE: *Josua 13–21.* Ein priesterschriftlicher Abschnitt im deuteronomistischen Geschichtswerk. 136 Seiten. 1990.

Bd. 95 ERIK HORNUNG (Herausgeber): *Zum Bild Ägyptens im Mittelalter und in der Renaissance. Comment se représente-t-on l'Egypte au Moyen Age et à la Renaissance.* 268 Seiten. 1990.

Bd. 96 ANDRÉ WIESE: *Zum Bild des Königs auf ägyptischen Siegelamuletten.* 264 Seiten. Mit zahlreichen Abbildungen im Text und 32 Tafeln. 1990.

Bd. 97 WOLFGANG ZWICKEL: *Räucherkult und Räuchergeräte.* Exegetische und archäologische Studien zum Räucheropfer im Alten Testament. 372 Seiten. Mit zahlreichen Abbildungen im Text. 1990.

Bd. 98 AARON SCHART: *Mose und Israel im Konflikt.* Eine redaktionsgeschichtliche Studie zu den Wüstenerzählungen. 296 Seiten. 1990.

Bd. 99 THOMAS RÖMER: *Israels Väter.* Untersuchungen zur Väterthematik im Deuteronomium und in der deuteronomistischen Tradition. 664 Seiten. 1990.

Bd. 100 OTHMAR KEEL / MENAKHEM SHUVAL / CHRISTOPH UEHLINGER: *Studien zu den Stempelsiegeln aus Palästina / Israel.* Band III. Die Frühe Eisenzeit. Ein Workshop. XIV–456 Seiten. Mit zahlreichen Abbildungen im Text und 22 Tafeln. 1990.

Bd. 101 CHRISTOPH UEHLINGER: *Weltreich und «eine Rede».* Eine neue Deutung der sogenannten Turmbauerzählung (Gen 11,1–9). XVI–654 Seiten. 1990.

Bd. 102 BENJAMIN SASS: *Studia Alphabetica.* On the Origin and Early History of the Northwest Semitic, South Semitic and Greek Alphabets. X–120 Seiten. 16 Seiten Abbildungen. 2 Tabellen. 1991.

Bd. 103 ADRIAN SCHENKER: *Text und Sinn im Alten Testament.* Textgeschichtliche und bibeltheologische Studien. VIII–312 Seiten. 1991.

Bd. 104 DANIEL BODI: *The Book of Ezekiel and the Poem of Erra.* IV–332 Seiten. 1991.

Bd. 105 YUICHI OSUMI: *Die Kompositionsgeschichte des Bundesbuches Exodus 20,22b–23,33.* XII–284 Seiten. 1991.

Bd. 106 RUDOLF WERNER: *Kleine Einführung ins Hieroglyphen-Luwische.* XII–112 Seiten. 1991.

Bd. 107 THOMAS STAUBLI: *Das Image der Nomaden im Alten Israel und in der Ikonographie seiner sesshaften Nachbarn.* XII–408 Seiten. 145 Abb. und 3 Falttafeln. 1991.

Bd. 108 MOSHÉ ANBAR: *Les tribus amurrites de Mari.* VIII–256 Seiten. 1991.

Bd. 109 GÉRARD J. NORTON / STEPHEN PISANO (eds.): *Tradition of the Text.* Studies offered to Dominique Barthélemy in Celebration of his 70th Birthday. 336 Seiten. 1991.

Bd. 110 HILDI KEEL-LEU: *Vorderasiatische Stempelsiegel.* Die Sammlung des Biblischen Instituts der Universität Freiburg Schweiz. 180 Seiten. 24 Tafeln. 1992.

Bd. 111 NORBERT LOHFINK: *Die Väter Israels im Deuteronomiun.* Mit einer Stellungnahme von Thomas Römer. 152 Seiten. 1991.

Bd. 112 EDMUND HERMSEN: *Die zwei Wege des Jenseits*. Das altägyptische Zweiwegebuch und seine Topographie. XII–282 Seiten, 1 mehrfarbige und 19 schwarzweiss-Abbildungen. 1992.

Bd. 113 CHARLES MAYSTRE: *Les grands prêtres de Ptah de Memphis*. XIV–474 pages, 2 planches. 1992.

Bd. 114 SCHNEIDER THOMAS: *Asiatische Personennamen in Ägyptischen Quellen des Neuen Reiches*. 208 Seiten. 1992.

Bd. 115 VON NORDHEIM ECKHARD: *Die Selbstbehauptung Israels in der Welt des Alten Orients*. Religionsgeschichtlicher Vergleich anhand von Gen 15/22/28, dem Aufenthalt Israels in Ägypten, 2 Sam 7, 1 Kön 19 und Psalm 104. 240 Seiten. 1992.

Bd. 116 DONALD M. MATTHEWS: *The Kassite Glyptic of Nippur*. 208 Seiten. 210 Abbildungen. 1992.

Bd. 117 FIONA V. RICHARDS: *Scarab Seals from a Middle to Late Bronze Age Tomb at Pella in Jordan*. XII–152 Seiten, 16 Tafeln. 1992.

UNIVERSITÄTSVERLAG FREIBURG SCHWEIZ

*Summary*

The site of Pella of the Decapolis, located in the Jordan Valley, has been excavated under the auspices of the University of Sydney, Australia. The project has revealed an extensive multi-period site with an impressive coverage of the Bronze Age. Tomb 62, a Middle to Late Bronze Age tomb, is the richest discovered at the site and one of the largest in the Levant.

This catalogue of the scarabs from Tomb 62 comprises a large and unique collection from a closed context. It offers a typological, chronological, historical and comparative survey. Ward and Tufnell's pioneering classification system is utilized and modified to incorporate previously unknown types from the Pella collection.

Essentially, this catalogue provides valuable comparative material and contributes to our understanding of the complex interplay between Egypt and Palestine in the Hyksos period.